PALM BEACH CHIC

PALM
BEACH
CHIC

JENNIFER ASH RUDICK

PHOTOGRAPHY BY
JESSICA KLEWICKI GLYNN

VENDOME

NEW YORK

CONTENTS

INTRODUCTION

A LIFELONG FASCINATION WITH HOUSES OF ALL KINDS began with my first trip to Palm Beach. It was a reconnaissance mission—there was a possibility that the island would be my family's new home. I was twelve years old and not eager to move, but as our car crested the "middle bridge," revealing a tropical allée of towering royal palms and meticulously tended flower beds dividing the wide boulevard, Royal Palm Way, my resistance melted away. We drove along South Ocean Boulevard, where the mansions seemed as mysterious as mad King Ludwig's castles. Mar-a-Lago, El Solano, Casa Nana, and Il Palmetto lined the thoroughfare like imperial ladies on a receiving line.

Our first stop was Worth Avenue, then anchored by a gas station and the Colony Hotel with its tilting carport. Saks Fifth Avenue was the dominant retailer. The store was fashioned after a Venetian palazzo, with polished marble floors and a curving double staircase lined with ornamental cast-iron balusters. The Arctic air conditioning blasted hurricane-force winds of Arpège, the perfume craze of the era. Tempting merchandise, interspersed with tropical symbols—seashells and polished-brass sand pails—was sparsely arrayed on gilded tables. There were sharply creased white sharkskin shorts and ribbed Courrèges sweaters in icy pastels. The store was an authoritative reflection of what I assumed was life in Palm Beach—chic, tropical, upbeat.

I followed my parents through a bougainvillea-covered archway into Via Mizner, entering a colorful shop hardly larger than the pushcart filled with crates of oranges that served as the doorstop. My mother introduced me to her fabric-turbaned Key West pal Lilly Pulitzer. Nearby, I spotted a tombstone dedicated to a pet monkey and not far away a water fountain for dogs cemented to the sidewalk. "Palm Beachers love their animals," my father noted. I thought I might be able to live here.

After an outdoor lunch at Testa's Palm Beach restaurant, we met a real estate agent. She guided us through Mediterranean Revivals, Colonials, Bermudas, and Regencies. The interiors ran the gamut: simple, ornate, cluttered, spare, ramshackle, and those with every screw at a forty-five-degree angle. Some were modest, others magnificent,

OPPOSITE: The pool pavilion in Kit Pannill's north garden is shaded by an enormous *Ficus benjamina.*

ABOVE: Breakfast served with a copy of the *Palm Beach Daily News* is an island tradition.

ABOVE: The decoratively carved and painted door of a guesthouse at the home of Katharine and William Rayner.

OPPOSITE: The morning room at La Follia.

and I could easily imagine myself living happily in any one of them. I sensed that my parents felt the same way, but we kept looking. My mother explained that house hunting was the best way to gain insight into the social patterns of an insular town. Each had a backstory revealing the tastes, penchants, exotic travels, and idiosyncrasies of the inhabitants. Their lives were stocked with antiques, monogrammed linens, elaborate fish aquariums, and pillows needlepointed with cautionary slogans like "Guest of guest may not bring guest." I understood that a certain segment of the population would tap the most obscure connection to snag an invitation to Palm Beach.

From my adult perspective today, I realize that Palm Beach was basically what it had always been—the land of dreams come true, a world of imaginatively designed and quality-built nesting places. High tray ceilings, proper entrance halls, excellent proportions, a sense of propriety, but not a trace of competitive consumption. Palm Beachers lived graciously but with individual interpretations of the concept.

In the end, my parents selected a simple CBS (concrete block structure) house designed by Michael Burrows, a beloved hometown architect, perhaps because it reminded them of our Miami house. A single level, well constructed with good proportions, windows open to the blazing sunlight. My mother swathed our living room in a Brunschwig & Fils tulip-patterned waxy chintz and placed a grassy green, custom-made Edward Fields rug underfoot. Needlepoint cushions designed by Lou Gartner nestled in every upholstered corner.

Denis Lamarsh designed a garden that transformed our small property into a tropical escape. "Palm Beach is more lighthearted, more resort oriented than Miami," my mother observed. Just having been named publisher of the *Palm Beach Daily News*, she doubled down on this perception, ordering all the paper's sidewalk circulation boxes to be painted Mizner pink, a color closely identified with the town's most revered architect, Addison Mizner.

In time, I came to consider the island my home. I had my first kiss on the balcony of the Joseph Urban–designed Paramount Theatre and my first job was at an ice cream store, where my friends helped me eat all my earnings. I felt very much the local when giving visitors the real estate tour, the same tour my parents had given me all those years ago.

I always opened with the showstoppers, including Mar-a-Lago, created in 1927 by architect and set designer Joseph Urban for cereal heiress Marjorie Merriweather Post, which morphed into Donald Trump's private club; Bethesda-by-the-Sea Episcopal Church; St. Edward Church, where the Kennedys worshipped; the magnificent Whitehall, home of oil and railroad tycoon Henry Flagler and his youthful third wife. Along the way, I connected historical dots, explaining that Flagler turned the alligator-infested swamp known as Lake Worth into a tropical paradise featuring two palatial

Path through the "jungle"
surrounding the Lauder house.

hotels and accessed by his railway line, which included a siding for parking private railroad cars upholstered in fringed red velvet. When Flagler's original Breakers hotel burned down, his wealthy widow replaced it with an even more formidable structure.

Since its early days, Palm Beach has been synonymous with awe-inspiring structures. But on my tours I tried to tell it like it was. I introduced my guests to the simple pleasures of milkshakes at Green's Pharmacy, chilly views of surfers on the beach at the end of Reef Road, and tiny, slightly tilted cabanas shared by residents on the island's North End streets leading to the ocean.

Of course, everyone always asked, "What's behind the hedges?" In response, I took visitors to the bike path, where, at that time, every house was on display. Eventually, I was given the opportunity to address that very question professionally in the book *Private Palm Beach: Tropical Style.* The publisher understood that Palm Beach wasn't all mansions filled with gilded furniture and agreed that the book should reflect the varied ways of life on that most private of private islands, including not only mansions and landmarked homes but also apartments, cottages, and new builds—all transformative and each the best of the best. These homes attested to the fact that Palm Beachers were observant, sophisticated world travelers who entertained crowned heads and even those who had given up their crowns. The architecture reflected lifestyles restricted only by imagination, not by income. *Private Palm Beach* captured the resort's architectural ambience as it was in 1992, when the book was originally published. Now the time has come to have another look.

Like the rest of the world, Palm Beach has changed. South Ocean Boulevard, once affectionately called "Millionaire's Row" is now called "Billionaire's Row." Real estate on the barrier island has become increasingly valuable. A house must be worthy of the price of the land on which it is anchored. American fortunes are still being made and maintained, but those who hold them are more inclined to call in experts when it comes to creating their mansions. This is, after all, the age of specialization.

When the first book was published, new edifices had not challenged the imperial ladies of the 1920s. But in the mid-1990s, along came a complex designed by Jeff Smith with interiors by Pauline Pitt and gardens by Mario Nievera. Named La Follia, it was the brainchild of its owner, Broadway producer Terry Allen Kramer, and it signaled the start of a new building boom.

The homes on the following pages show the remarkable results that can be achieved through the blending of professional skill, unfettered imagination, and the natural beauty of the subtropics. There are sinuous midcentury modern apartments, cozy cottages, postmodern houses, and romantic Regencies, each of which reflects the tastes, passions, and whimsies of the individuals who call it home. Fashion designer Josie Natori asked architect Calvin Tsao to transform a simple two-bedroom condominium into an airy retreat with rattan furniture and objets d'art reflecting her Asian heritage. A postmodern aesthetic reigns in the homes of art patron Beth DeWoody and designer Lisa Perry.

Two of the houses have remained in the same families for half a century. Villa Artemis, owned by the Horvitz family, was recently rejuvenated by the dream team of architect Mark Ferguson, designer David Kleinberg, and landscape designer Mario Nievera. The Old Bethesda-by-the-Sea Church remains in the family of Mimi McMakin, whose forebears deconsecrated it, and members of the family have been living there since the 1940s, using the church nave as a catch-all for the free-spirited family's assorted oddities.

The first book featured the home of the late Lilly Pulitzer, the epitome of the innovative, easy-going, high-achieving Palm Beacher, who had created a veritable jungle around her compound. Her daughter Liza's own compound is equally buoyant and welcoming. A lakeside cottage that once belonged to Liza's father, Peter Pulitzer, has been brought back to life for a family by local designer extraordinaire Lillian Fernandez. Amado, which appeared in *Private Palm Beach* when it was owned by Dorothy Spreckels Munn, appears here in a completely transformed state, thanks to the new owners, who hired designer David Easton and garden designer John Lang.

Trunk of a huge
Ficus benjamina.

Easton is fond of saying, "There is no great house without a great garden." That has never been more true than it is in Palm Beach today. Never have interiors and the surrounding grounds been more closely integrated. For that reason, this book includes a section on gardens, including Kit Pannill's spectacular new greenhouse, designed by Leta Austin Foster. Kit isn't at all perturbed when friends refer to her as the reigning queen of Palm Beach gardening.

Garden designers have become celebrities. Horticulture hasn't been so hot since Frederick Law Olmsted created Manhattan's Central Park. Jorge Sánchez, Alan Stopek, and Mario Nievera are the masterminds behind the greening of the town's public spaces. Stopek's private projects include the oasis he created for Garden Club president Vicky Hunt; Nievera designed the grounds for a number of the houses in the book, as did Sánchez, whose own otherworldly ranch, located not far beyond the island's bridges, is also featured.

The Preservation Foundation of Palm Beach created the Lesly S. Smith Landscape Award to recognize excellence in landscape design. Smith, an advocate of preserving and enhancing public and private gardens—and once the mayor of Palm Beach—is the widow of longtime mayor Earl E. T. Smith. (While I was working on the book, her daughter, Danielle Hickox Moore, became a town councilwoman, thus establishing a Palm Beach political dynasty.) The gardens of two of the houses in the book are recipients of this prestigious award: one is Villa Artemis and the other is the home of Katharine and William Rayner, whose gardens were designed by Denis Lamarsh and Michael Peasley in the Moroccan and Persian styles.

A prime example of a revived garden is that of Estée Lauder's oceanfront home, originally built by a Florida banking tycoon. It is now owned by the cosmetics pioneer's son Leonard Lauder, who called upon landscape designer Mario Nievera to create a junglelike ambience that has softened the exterior and makes the property more conducive to outdoor living.

These homes and their magnificent gardens aren't slavish copies of interior design magazines or decorators' dictates but testaments to what can be achieved when inspired by the natural beauty of a unique locale and when imagination is one's only limitation.

LA FOLLIA

TERRY ALLEN KRAMER'S REMARKABLE BROADWAY RUN includes producer credits for the smash hits *Elephant Man*, *Kinky Boots*, *Movin' Out*, *Me and My Girl*, and *Sugar Babies*. But her most extraordinary and enduring production to date remains the creation of La Follia—a 43,000-square-foot Italian Renaissance–style dream house, completed in 1995. If Addison Mizner's El Mirasol, a Spanish Colonial Revival mansion built in 1919 for socialite Eva Stotesbury, turned Palm Beach into a preeminent winter playground for the international beau monde, then it was the creation of La Follia that ushered in Palm Beach's next mansion boom.

When Kramer and her late husband, financier Irwin Kramer, decamped from Lyford Cay in the Bahamas to Palm Beach, she considered the inventory of available historic mansions but craved twentieth-century amenities and more light than those on offer provided. Instead, she purchased a 3.7-acre oceanfront lot that was elevated enough to afford views of the Intracoastal Waterway across the island and began to think about what to construct. A house on the grand scale of Kramer's imaginings hadn't been built in over seven decades, but that didn't deter her—thinking big is Kramer's specialty.

Kramer gave architect Jeff Smith, interior designer Pauline Pitt, and landscape designer Mario Nievera twenty-two months to turn a perfectly sited but overgrown lot into a showcase worthy of her vision. Last call for construction was November 1, 1995, in time for the house's official opening on Thanksgiving Day.

Architect Jeff Smith's lifeblood is historic buildings; his impeccable restorations, including that of Palm Beach Town Hall, put him on the map, but until La Follia, he had never built such a large house from the ground up. Nonetheless, Kramer put her faith in him, handing over a six-page wish list. She wanted to blur the lines between indoors and outdoors, so Smith incorporated oversized windows and plenty of loggias and terraces. The nod to Broadway is an enormous plate-glass window, set on elevator pylons, that slides into the floor, transforming a protected indoor loggia into an ocean-side terrace.

OPPOSITE: The entrance hall is clad in the same white coquina as the house's façade, creating a seamless transition between inside and out. The enfilade of archways beyond marks a 106-foot-long great hall featuring a groin-vaulted ceiling. This hall provides access to all the ground-floor rooms and the western terrace. A Venetian-patterned floor is composed of three types of marble: creamy Botticino, green Verde; and red Rosso Alicante.

ABOVE: Orchids add splashes of color throughout the house and gardens.

Interior designer Pauline Pitt's own Palm Beach heritage dates back to the 1920s, when her grandfather Charles "Mr. Palm Beach" Munn commissioned Mizner to build the seaside mansion Amado. Moreover, Pitt worked with Kramer on her New York and Southampton houses; she knew her client's taste and how to translate it into interiors appropriate for Palm Beach living. "Terry likes walking through the house barefoot," Pitt says, "yet the house is slightly formal because she had been in Lyford and this felt like coming to the city for her." In other words, the house had to be grand enough for a seated dinner for 150 that Kramer would host for the Duke of Marlborough's birthday but still cozy enough for a family with six grandchildren, who would spend weekends running through the house from the beach to the pool.

Pitt's first order was a handmade living room carpet from Stark that would take nineteen months to arrive and on which she based the pale blue, yellow, mauve, and green palette. She added playful touches such as curtain rods with gilded bird finials.

Meanwhile, Nievera worked on gardens that would frame the house, enhance the views, and provide a play area for the children. "Terry had an image of an Italian garden with four quadrants and a fountain in the middle," he says. "We planted three hundred rose bushes. Every year she got a great yield, which isn't easy in Florida." A lawn in the courtyard was designed for the grandchildren to play on, and the pool was surrounded with a combination of grass and coquina for drainage and for softness under bare feet.

As November approached, the team picked up the pace. The finishing touches of painters, electricians, plumbers, carpenters, and gardeners went off without a hitch, the deadline was met, and the house opened to rave reviews. La Follia received an Award for Excellence from the American Institute of Architects, Palm Beach Chapter. It was the talk of the town and to this day, everyone wants an invitation to the house that turned the spotlight back on this barrier island.

BELOW: The 34-by-44-foot living room is used for formal entertaining. The Italian Renaissance–style coffered ceiling and stone cornice and door surrounds provide grandeur, while the sea foam–colored walls and fabrics in shades of pale mauve, blue, green, and yellow, echoing the hues of the custom-designed carpet, imbue the room with an airy and whimsical spirit.

OPPOSITE: The owner's favorite Picassos flank the massive stone fireplace.

OPPOSITE: The library's knotty pine paneling is ornamented with intricate Renaissance-style carving executed by local craftsmen. Beyond the library are the loggia, living room, and morning room. In the loggia, glass windows, set on elevator pylons, can be lowered underground to create an open-air, ocean-side terrace.

ABOVE: An atrium with fancifully tiled walls connects the dining room, morning room, and kitchen. The dining room features butter-yellow, textured-linen walls and English pedestal tables.

OPPOSITE AND ABOVE: An arched breezeway connects four guest rooms to the main house. Each guest room has its own lush outdoor courtyard, complete with a trickling fountain. The blue guest room is decorated with a cheerful oversized poppy print from Brunschwig & Fils in two colorways. The breezeway, ornamented with hand-painted tiles, can be seen through the window above the armchair and ottoman.

TOP: The yellow guest room features a handmade bed with bamboo posts from Wilhelm's Rattan.

OVERLEAF: The morning room is reminiscent of an old-fashioned orangerie. Palladian-style arched doors open onto the Atlantic Ocean. The trelliswork walls, à la Elsie de Wolfe, and the octagonal rug, featuring macaws, monkeys, and tropical flowers, add to the room's charm. The round ivory table is from Colombia.

ABOVE: La Follia's exterior walls are clad in coquina, which has turned from its original white to the desired sandy beige. Stone arches, supported by Corinthian columns, define three sides of the west terrace, which overlooks a grassy courtyard.

OPPOSITE: The west terrace is a favorite lunch spot. Corbels carved with acanthus leaves embellish the coffered ceiling.

OVERLEAF: Eighteenth-century blue-and-white chinoiserie plates cemented to the wall add warmth to the space. The rattan furniture is from Wilhelm's. The courtyard of the yellow guest room can be seen beyond the terrace. Enormous pots of orchids add splashes of color to the garden.

PAGES 32–33: View of the courtyard and pool from the west terrace. Two guest rooms, connected by outdoor corridors, flank the courtyard. La Follia's twenty-four-foot elevation permits a view of the Intracoastal Waterway beyond the pool. To the left of the pool, a ligustrum tree is hung with orchids. Hans, the family's German shorthaired pointer, stands guard.

OPPOSITE: Large arched windows and breezeways lighten the estate's formal Italianate ocean-side façade. Completed in 1995, the house was one of the grandest and most admired mansions built in Palm Beach since the 1920s' boom and was a forerunner of the town's twenty-first-century Renaissance.

TOP LEFT: This section of the parterre-style formal garden is edged in boxwood and planted with mona lavender and geraniums.

TOP RIGHT: A stone lion guards the sloping lawn leading to the Atlantic Ocean.

ABOVE: The west side of the house overlooks the parterre, which is flanked by citrus and banyan trees. Low hedges and beds of flowers and foliage border the fountains and the brick-accented path, which winds through the property.

POSTMODERNIST PERFECTION

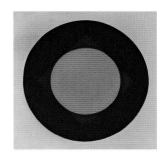

Nestled in a stretch of oceanfront labeled Billionaires' Row for its lineup of opulent mansions is designer Lisa Perry's version of a surf shack—a stark-white, low-lying alternate reality in both magnitude and geometry.

For years, Lisa and her husband, financier Richard Perry, kept an apartment in Palm Beach. But passing a doorman every day didn't spell vacation—the couple lives that way in New York City. They craved a transformative spot where they could paddleboard and dine ocean-side out their back door. Real estate sleuthing by bicycle—a favorite Palm Beach diversion—progressed to calling a realtor. Two weeks later they found their dream house. "You walk in the front door and see straight through the living room to the ocean. It takes my breath away every time."

The house was built on spec in 1985 by Palm Beach developer Robert Gottfried. Inspired by the neoclassical buildings he had admired in Paris and motivated to make a name for himself on the Palm Beach real estate scene, which had long been dominated by Mediterranean Revival, Gottfried began designing Regency-style houses, eventually building some five hundred residences. Complete with stucco swags and urn-shaped finials, Gottfried's homes are still prominent on the streets he developed, including Chateaux Drive, El Dorado Lane, El Mirasol, and Via Los Incas.

Naturally, when it came to conceiving her house, Perry brought the exacting eye evident in her fashion line, which boasts architectural cuts with fearless splashes of color—à la Courrèges. "I know what I like." Perry's unshakable aesthetic was formed early, in part by her childhood home outside of Chicago, which was designed by a Frank Lloyd Wright protégé.

Gottfried's clean lines and airy atmosphere appealed to Perry but not the Regency embellishments. "I asked our architect, Christine Harper, to take everything down to a white box," she says. Perry planned the interiors around an extensive Modernist and

OPPOSITE: The spirit of Perry's bright and sunny home extends to an ocean-side outdoor shower.

ABOVE: A detail of a Kenneth Noland's painting *Indent*.

Postmodernist art and furniture collection, including works by Kenneth Noland, Damien Hirst, and Vladimir Kagan. An enormous crescent-shaped white leather sofa by de Sede is the centerpiece of the living room, where it faces the show-stopping ocean view that continues to mesmerize everyone who visits. Perry concedes, "It isn't really a beach shack, but it functions like one with its seamless movement from inside out."

OPPOSITE: The entrance offers a dramatic view straight through the living room to the Atlantic Ocean.

RIGHT: A detail of the painted tile that edges the pavement in front of the house.

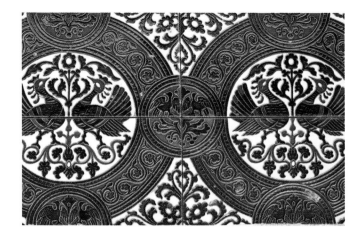

ABOVE: A painting by Doug Ohlson and a light fixture by Raimond Puts from B&B Italia decorate the entrance hall.

OVERLEAF: The house was designed by Florida developer Robert Gottfried in 1985. Perry's beloved palm trees dot the property.

ABOVE: Chaises longues from Sifas
are lined up facing the ocean.

OPPOSITE: The house sits on 145
feet of Atlantic Ocean beachfront.

OVERLEAF: The den overlooks
the pool and the ocean beyond.
Monochrome paintings by Tadaaki
Kuwayama hang above the sofa and
ottoman, which were designed by
Francesco Binfaré. The chairs are
by Pierre Paulin for Ligne Roset.
Lisa Perry designed the pillows.

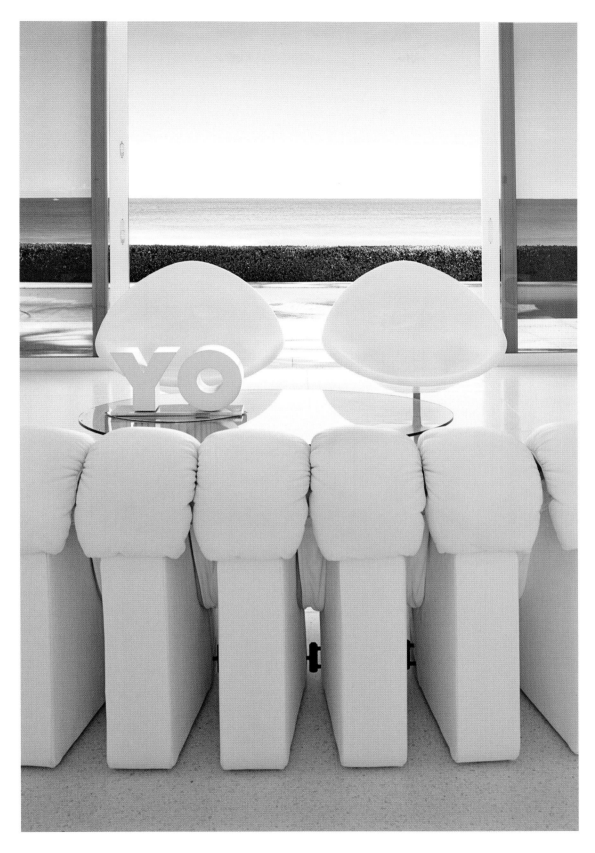

PRECEDING PAGES: Damien Hirst's *Elaidyl Alcohol* hangs on the living room wall leading into the den. The hall leading to a bedroom is decorated with Charles Hinman's *Diagonal Split* on the left and *Total Eclipse Yellow* on the right. At the end of the hall is Tadaaki Kuwayama's *TK48-03*.

OPPOSITE AND ABOVE: The living room is anchored by a crescent-shaped white leather sofa by de Sede. The vintage chairs are by Pierre Paulin. The sculpture on the glass-topped table is *OY/YO* by Deborah Kass. Perry chose terrazzo for the floors throughout most of the house.

OPPOSITE: The kitchen is painted in Benjamin Moore's Regal in Chantilly Lace. The cabinets are custom made, and the counters are topped with Corian. The stools were found in Belgium.

ABOVE LEFT: Four plates by Nicolas Party.

ABOVE RIGHT: In the dining room, armchairs by Georg Appeltshauser surround a vintage table. The hanging lamp is by Davide Groppi. The series of vertical gray paintings are by Tadaaki Kuwayama.

FAR LEFT: An Eero Saarinen Womb chair and ottoman sit in a corner of a guest room.

LEFT: In the master bedroom, Kenneth Noland's painting *Indent* hangs above a bench by Guglielmo Ulrich.

BELOW: Noland's painting *Florio* hangs above the bed, which was designed by Patricia Urquiola. The desk, by Angelo Mangiarotti, is accompanied by an acrylic Philippe Starck chair. The yellow chair is by Pierre Paulin.

OPPOSITE: An "Op Gown" from Lisa Perry's Fall 2013 collection hangs in the dressing room area. The tub in the master bathroom overlooks a garden.

OPPOSITE: In a guest room, a painting by Damien Hirst hangs above a vintage chair that Perry found in a shop on Dixie Highway in West Palm Beach.

ABOVE: In the same room, Leon Polk Smith's *Big Space— Black Line* is mounted over the bed.

COTTAGES

THE GRAND, SUN-DAPPLED MEDITERRANEAN MANSIONS lining South Ocean Boulevard will always be emblematic of Palm Beach, but the island's first house was a modest cottage built entirely of surf debris. Settlers of the Lake Worth Cottage Colony—Palm Beach's original name until a cargo of coconuts was salvaged from a wrecked Spanish brigantine and planted, rebranding the island—consisted of about nineteen families vacationing in modest clapboard structures that tilted in the tides washing the eastern banks of Lake Worth. Two of those structures still stand side by side; Duck's Nest, brought from Brooklyn by barge in 1891, and the original Bethesda-by-the-Sea Church, whose enormous Shingle Style tower, with its Seth Thomas clock, dominates the Intracoastal shoreline, fascinating those who spot it from the nearby bike path.

Other turn-of-the-century cottages are squeezed gable to gable along Root Trail, as well as along Seabreeze, Seaspray, and Seaview Avenues. Whimsical Victorian or boxy New England in style, the cottages share many of the same design traits as their grander neighbors, including foyers, dining rooms, beamed ceilings, bedroom wings, and even miniature guesthouses, all designed with nutshell efficiency. Their decoration is usually charmingly idiosyncratic, imbued with style and verve.

GEORGIAN REDUX

Palm Beach's newer British Colonial and Caribbean-style houses share design basics introduced in the mid-1920s by architect Howard Major. Major studied at the New York Atelier of Beaux-Arts; as chief draftsman for architect Charles Alonzo Rich, he designed a building at Dartmouth College and country houses for Long Island socialites. He arrived in Palm Beach during the booming 1920s and landed a job with Addison Mizner. His boss was in command of the beach colony's preference for Mediterranean Revival

OPPOSITE: An intimate cluster of six buildings affectionately known as Major Alley, built in the mid-1920s, remains the most visible and beloved testament to architect Howard Major's Caribbean Colonial vision.

ABOVE: Detail of a painting by Roberto Juarez that hangs in the master bedroom of Liza Pulitzer's North End cottage.

architecture, a style that clients became infatuated with after culture-harvesting trips to Europe, so Major carved an identity for himself by designing Georgian-style houses modified for the subtropical climate, taking cues from the Bahamas, Jamaica, and Bermuda.

Many of his prominent mansions, including 235 Banyan Road and 135 El Vedado Road, still stand, having been protected by the Palm Beach Landmarks Preservation Commission. Equally vociferously defended is an intimate cluster of six cottages known as Major Alley. Built in the mid-1920s, the Alley is a treasured testament to Major's vision of Georgian redux.

BELOW: The owners found fish sculptures in a shop on West Palm Beach's Dixie Highway and had them simonized to withstand the elements.

RIGHT: A walkway to the main house in the Major Alley complex is adorned with orchids.

OPPOSITE: An office, hung with a Rose Cumming banana-leaf wallpaper, opens onto the courtyard pool.

OPPOSITE: Afternoon sunlight shines into the west-facing entrance hall.

ABOVE: "Mistletoe" hangs year round.

RIGHT: In the dining room, the interior of a cupboard was painted a cheery coral. The wallpaper is from Cole & Son. The lily-pad plates on the wall are from Global Views.

BELOW: To lend contemporary flair to the living room, the designer, Lori Deeds of Kemble Interiors, selected a Donghia Bond Street Sofa. Pillows are covered in Raoul's "Secret Garden" fabric. The vintage faux goatskin coffee table is by Karl Springer, circa 1975. The owner found a pair of glass-fronted cabinets on Dixie Highway.

TOP LEFT: Detail of the shell-encrusted fireplace surround in the living room of Jean Pearman's guest cottage in Major Alley.

CENTER LEFT: A cozy courtyard, its walls trellised with vines, is a favorite lunch spot.

BOTTOM LEFT: A fountain rescued from a nearby Mizner house decorates the courtyard of the Pearman guest cottage.

ABOVE: For the living room walls, designer Mimi Kemble and Jean Pearman chose a shimmering, and inviting, cantaloupe glaze. White upholstery keeps the room airy, while chocolate brown trim sets off the owner's antique furniture crisply. Matchstick blinds under white curtains are one of Kemble's favorite Florida window treatments.

OVERLEAF LEFT AND RIGHT: Climbing bougainvillea and planted window boxes are among Major Alley's most recognizable features.

TROPICAL COMPOUND

Liza Pulitzer Calhoun's exuberant design philosophy is based on disguising the foibles of animals and children. "Prints work for us. I don't want to worry if a dog jumps up on the furniture or a child eats peanut butter on the sofa. Peter, Minnie, and I have always lived that way," says Calhoun, referring to her brother and sister, who reside nearby. The siblings' shared aesthetic was passed down to them from their beloved mother, Lilly Pulitzer, whose neon-colored prints defined an era. "She threw in antique pieces with fake banana plants. There was never a formula. Mom taught us to be fearless with color and fearless in life."

Whereas Lilly preferred bright florals, Liza favors saturated African, Indian, and other ethnic prints. "I consider eggplant a neutral color," says Calhoun, who transformed two rundown 1920s cottages into an airy compound. The cottages' pitched roofs, louvered windows, ceiling fans, and painted-wood floors reference childhood vacations spent in the Bahamas. The heart of the compound is an outdoor living room conjured up by Liza and her husband, Bob, as a way to connect the cottages. Only in extreme hot or cold do the Calhouns retreat to the indoor family room. The original living room, at the front of the main house, is now a dining room.

"Palm Beach has a reputation for being strictly formal. But that's not the case with people who live here year round. We put a buffet in the kitchen and everyone gathers by the outdoor fireplace." For a time, Lilly's kitchen and slat house were the epicenter of Palm Beach, and the hostess never wore shoes. Calhoun carries on the tradition, perpetuating the relaxed Pulitzer legacy. "There's always food on the table and drinks in the bar. People come and go and everyone is welcome," she says.

Perennials envelop the front porch. A canvas-weave fabric that withstands the elements and the assaults of numerous pets covers the cushions of the wicker furniture.

TOP: A photo of a young Lilly and Peter Pulitzer.

ABOVE: A white wooden mantel pops against lime green walls. A fish-eye mirror reflects the whole room.

ABOVE: A custom-made chandelier that is also a wind chime hangs over the large, rustic dining room table. Liza's sister, Minnie McCluskey, and a friend painted all the floors and walls in the compound; they chose lime green for the dining room walls. The diamond pattern on the floor was done freehand. A painting by A. Steven Witt contributes to the tropical atmosphere.

TOP, LEFT TO RIGHT: A photo of Liza as a young girl captures a childhood spent barefoot in Palm Beach and the Bahamas; like her mother, Liza loves colorful prints but prefers warm tribal versions, including ikats; stacked vintage picnic baskets serve as an end table.

ABOVE: The twelve-foot-long kitchen island was fashioned from wood salvaged from the room's original ceiling. During dinner parties, it serves as a buffet. The photograph over the sofa is by Liza's son Christopher Leidy, an underwater photographer.

OPPOSITE: Liza's sister painted the kitchen walls tomato-soup red. She did the striped floor freehand, as Liza "doesn't do perfect."

OVERLEAF: An outdoor living room was devised to connect the main house and the guest cottage. The vaulted ceiling of cypress treated with a lime wash and the rattan furniture impart a tropical feel. A deep overhang protects the seating area from rain.

OPPOSITE: The fireplace in the outdoor living room is made of concrete embedded with stones, shells, and barnacles that Calhoun and her family collect from all over the world.

ABOVE, CLOCKWISE FROM TOP LEFT: The owner propagates orchids; sea fans from the nearby beach decorate the outdoor fireplace mantel; Liza displays stones and shells collected from trips to Kilimanjaro, Mongolia, Scotland, and the Palm Beach Inlet; the rattan furniture is from Palecek.

TOP LEFT: The plates displayed in the bar are Liza and Bob Calhoun's golf trophies.

TOP RIGHT: A watercolor of Lilly Pulitzer's first shop in Palm Beach's Via Mizner hangs above childhood photos.

ABOVE: The bar doubles as a family room when the weather is too hot or too cold to stay outdoors.

OPPOSITE: The vintage bar is painted to resemble pecky cypress. The tarpon was photographed by Calhoun's son Christopher Leidy on a free dive in the Palm Beach Inlet.

In the master bathroom, the faded-teal walls and soft gray-and-white floor provide a calming atmosphere for a luxuriant soak in the romantic claw-foot tub, a reproduction from Kallista.

The vintage bench was a gift from Calhoun's mother, Lilly Pulitzer.

OPPOSITE: The master bedroom overlooks the pool. The four-poster and gauzy bed curtains lend the room a breezy island feel. The floral bed cover is a repurposed tablecloth that once belonged to Lilly Pulitzer, A painting by Roberto Juarez references the compound's tropical garden.

LAKESIDE CHARM

No family was less bound by convention or more emblematic of Palm Beach's carefree '60s and '70s than the Pulitzer clan. Peter and Lilly's first lakeside clapboard home was a former boardinghouse—each bedroom door was boldly numbered. Parties ended up in the kitchen, where everyone watched Lilly cook. Forever imaginative and industrious, Lilly launched her eponymous dress line, modeling the psychedelic sheaths in her usual bare feet. Peter, an orange grove farmer, built a boat in their front yard. "The whole town came to help me launch it," he recalls. "Can you imagine that happening today?"

When the couple separated, Peter Pulitzer purchased an empty lakeside lot, built a dock, and moored to it a decrepit, engineless, 1923 houseboat he happily called home. Eventually, a town ordinance forced Pulitzer off the boat, so he built a house that defied Palm Beach standards: a deliberately modest post-and-beam structure that is difficult to categorize. "It was sort of a ranch house with exposed beams and air-conditioning ducts. The living room and kitchen were all one room," says Pulitzer, who lived there for fifteen years.

When real estate agent Crista Ryan, a descendant of another one of the island's great sporting families, heard that the house was on the market, her appreciation for the simple lakefront cottage proved contagious. Her clients not only purchased it but also turned to Crista's sister, interior designer Lillian Fernandez, to conjure up the interiors. Early in her career, Fernandez had restored the Vicarage, another historic lakeside cottage that had once belonged to Douglas Fairbanks Jr., to its original charm. With every house she's taken on around the world, Fernandez delivers a fresh perspective, and who would know better how to design an island home than a well-traveled

OPPOSITE: The dining room overlooks the pool and the Intracoastal Waterway beyond.

ABOVE: The handmade china is Dodie Thayer's Lettuce Ware, a classic Palm Beach look. Flowers here and throughout the house are by Lisa Bertles of LPB Orchids.

BELOW: Palms and ficus trees shade the pool to the west of the house.

RIGHT: The façade was refashioned to enhance the cottage feeling. Changes include the second-floor balcony and the tin roof.

OPPOSITE TOP: Fernandez loves mining local shops for furnishings, including a sofa from New Dimensions, Riviera Beach; a vintage Art Deco chaise from Valerio Antiques, Coral Gables; and a coffee table from Hive, West Palm Beach.

OPPOSITE BOTTOM: In the entrance hall, real bamboo trim is augmented with trompe l'oeil bamboo finish. Dark wood beams were pickled white. The owner's dog, Addie, absorbs the coolness of the stone floor.

local? "Palm Beach design is casual elegance, slightly more formal than the Bahamas but less fussy than a Northeastern beach house," she says.

Hired on October 1 and asked to have the rooms partially installed by Thanksgiving Day, Lillian suggested that the client meet her at North Carolina's High Point Market, where they could choose furniture in stock that could be put directly onto the delivery truck.

Since then, Fernandez and her client have been adding pieces from local sources to warm up the house and give it a Palm Beach soul. They scoured Dixie Highway shops and local galleries, including Leidy Images, where the client fell in love with Christopher Leidy's underwater photographs, purchasing more than a few. The fact that Leidy's work suited the house perfectly was no coincidence: the photographer is Peter and Lilly Pulitzer's grandson, another disciple of barefoot Palm Beach.

OPPOSITE: In the masculine yet airy library, the desk is by Dakota Jackson, the Art Deco chairs are from Randall Tysinger Antiques, the photograph of a library is by Massimo Listri from the Holden Luntz Gallery, Palm Beach, and the embroidered wall covering is by Phillip Jeffries.

RIGHT: The Palacek bar stools around the island in the kitchen are covered in Walfab fabric.

BELOW: The original dark ceiling in the family room was pickled and the floor was accented with a whimsical carpet from Barrier Island Rugs. The antique standing lamps are from F. S. Henemader, Palm Beach, and the Art Deco slipper chairs are from Randall Tysinger Antiques.

The master bedroom is a sophisticated pale gray with pops of yellow. The bed and night tables are from Century Furniture; the Art Deco coffee table is from Valerio Antiques, Coral Gables; all the upholstered furniture is from New Dimension, Riviera Beach, and the rattan desk and chairs are from Bamboo and Rattan, West Palm Beach.

A sunny guest room is swathed in a Manuel Canovas
palm-frond fabric. The antique rattan beds are
from Bamboo and Rattan, West Palm Beach.

STYLISH TRANQUILLITY

DAYS OF UNRELENTING RAIN SET IN MOTION HARRY and Laura Slatkin's quest for their dream house. "We couldn't shop along Worth Avenue one more time, so we called a real estate broker and decided to house-hunt instead," says Harry Slatkin. The Slatkins had been vacationing in Palm Beach for years and had occasionally looked at real estate, but nothing ever swept them off their feet. They had seen potential in a place they referred to as the "Gumdrop House" because its topiary trees reminded them of something out of Candy Land, but it was in need of an upgrade, and the couple, consumed with running a home fragrance company, weren't inclined to take on a renovation. "We come here to relax," says Laura Slatkin, who spent her childhood in Palm Beach, where her father was a society photographer.

When the real estate agent told them the Gumdrop House was back on the market, the Slatkins decided to have another look. Despite dark skies overhead, the house sparkled. "It had been transformed. It was beautiful and completely to our taste," says Laura.

The house was the work of legendary Palm Beach architect Marion Sims Wyeth, a 1910 graduate of Princeton University and a student at Paris's École des Beaux-Arts, who came to Palm Beach in 1919 and went on to design more than a hundred island houses in Georgian, French, and Colonial Revival styles, including the Moorish-style mansion Cielito Lindo for James and Jessie Woolworth Donahue, the ballroom of Mar-a-Lago for Marjorie Merriweather Post, the Norton Museum of Art, and the Florida Governor's mansion. In 1954 Wyeth was the first Palm Beach architect to be inducted into the American Institute of Architects (AIA), and he received the Test of Time Award from its Palm Beach Chapter in 1981.

The exterior of Gumdrop House is French in style; inside, the atmosphere is soothing and tranquil, consisting of predominantly neutral-hued rooms. The indoor spaces flow seamlessly into the property's lush, tropical garden, which is divided into intimate "rooms" by soaring walls of meticulously manicured Florida boxwood hedges.

OPPOSITE: The mirrored entrance hall reflects sunlight, bringing the outdoors in and creating the illusion of spaciousness.

ABOVE: Detail of the grass-outlined, diamond-patterned pavement of the driveway.

ABOVE: Gumdrop House is named after its topiary trees.

OPPOSITE: Lunch is a poolside buffet on the western loggia.

The living room is flanked by east and west loggias, and when the doors are thrown open, the house reads like an open-air pavilion; salt-filled breezes from the nearby Atlantic waft through every room. "As soon as we step into the house, we immediately decompress," says Harry.

Days are spent *en famille*. The mornings begin on the eastern loggia with coffee, as both Slatkins catch up on emails or read the papers. Tennis is at 11:30, followed by a buffet lunch at 1:30 on the western loggia. Afternoons are spent relaxing by the pool. Stormy weather no longer disrupts the Slatkins' vacations; if the skies cloud over, the family hunkers down in the library, which is equipped with over-stuffed chairs, a game table, and a big-screen television, and contentedly wait for the rain to pass.

TOP: The table, chairs, and cushions on the western loggia are by Rose Tarlow Melrose House. The curtains are made from Brunschwig & Fils cotton-linen duck cloth.

ABOVE: The pool area is enclosed by topiary hedges of Florida boxwood.

ABOVE: Fountains and glowing candles from NEST transform the pool into a water folly.

OVERLEAF: A tented loggia faces the garden to the east. The wicker furniture is by Bielecky Brothers. The nineteenth-century side tables were found at the Drouot auction house in Paris. The awning and curtains are duck cloth.

OPPOSITE TOP: Loggias on either side of the house (foreground and background) turn the interior into an airy pavilion.

OPPOSITE BOTTOM AND ABOVE: The Slatkins have gradually been introducing their own possessions into the mix, including fine pieces of blue-and-white Chinese export porcelain and an extensive collection of design and art books.

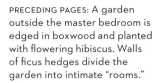

PRECEDING PAGES: A garden outside the master bedroom is edged in boxwood and planted with flowering hibiscus. Walls of ficus hedges divide the garden into intimate "rooms."

TOP LEFT, TOP RIGHT, AND ABOVE: The south-facing dining room opens onto a terrace and features a set of sixteen late seventeenth-century engravings of Indian flora compiled by Hendrik Adriaan van Rheede Tot Draakestein, acquired from Dinan & Chighine, London.

ABOVE: A terrace connecting the dining room and the kitchen is set for lunch. Hibiscus blossoms, plucked from the garden, decorate the table. Fountains on the east, west, and south sides of the house contribute to the soothing atmosphere.

OPPOSITE AND TOP LEFT: In the master bathroom, hand-printed towels, washcloths, bath mats, cushion, and robe in the "Fragrance" pattern are by D. Porthault. The monogrammed bath mat is from interior designer Leta Austin Foster's boutique in Via Mizner.

TOP RIGHT: The guest room is decorated with sailors' valentines—shell mosaics created on Barbados by local craftsmen in the nineteenth century. Sailors would bring them home from their voyages as gifts for their loved ones.

ABOVE: The bedding is by E. Braun & Company.

BAMBOO HILL

IN THE PROCESS OF ACQUIRING EXTRAORDINARY THINGS and the houses in which to display them, it's hard to determine where Swedish designer Lars Bolander's passion ends and his obsession begins. While traveling in France years ago, Bolander and his wife, artist Nadine Kalachnikoff, became so smitten with the Dordogne region that they decided to purchase a place on the spot. During a search in wretched weather, the clouds lifted, revealing a small château nestled in a grove of cedars. "We felt it was a sign, so we found the architect who created it. He was Turkish but spoke fluent Swedish. So we bought it. Of course we never lived in it. We didn't really have the time even to visit."

Making instant, life-enhancing decisions comes naturally to Bolander. He once sold a life insurance policy so he could purchase two eighteenth-century Belgian panels discovered at the Maastricht art fair. "When I was told they came from a house in the rue du Cirque in Paris, where my mother-in-law had an apartment, I had to have them."

These panels now hang on the luminous gray walls of an airy great room that is filled with other finds, including creamy white twentieth-century French settees, Gustavian end tables, Venetian consoles, a life-size tree sculpture, architectural Indian columns, and a sofa from the collection of Gunter Sachs. The room is a testament to Bolander's gift for creating perfectly scaled, tranquil interiors brimming with interesting objects of varying pedigree.

"There are no rules in design. It's fantasy and how you put it together." Bolander's impeccable instinct is rooted in a Swedish upbringing and formalized by studies at the Stockholm School of Art. He later worked with Swedish furniture designer Carl Malmsten and British interior designer Gaby Schreiber. He designed properties worldwide for industrialist Gunter Sachs before opening an antiques shop in the 1980s in East Hampton, a forerunner to stores in New York and later Palm Beach, prompting the couple to move to Florida. They first settled in an apartment overlooking Worth Avenue, and its enormous terrace soon became Palm Beach's social heartbeat.

OPPOSITE: A breezeway leading from the entrance hall to the back garden is decorated with carved-wood antlers. The chairs were found at Richard Mishaan's shop, Homer.

ABOVE: A wooden horse from Tibet stands in the open-air entrance hall of Bamboo Hill.

Bolander eventually purchased property in West Palm Beach, once part of a former orchid farm, where he designed the house of his dreams—his wish list included soaring ceilings, conjoined rooms, and enormous verandas. "I wanted all rooms to be open—even the library. I'm very tall, and I was never comfortable in small rooms," he observes. Bolander sketched out a dramatic, two-story-high great room, as much to accommodate his height as his large, rotating collection. "Things come bit by bit, not all in one go," he explains.

Bedroom suites are situated off balconies at either end of the great room. The kitchen and a guest room flank the south and north ends of the east-facing loggia, where Lars and Nadine spend most of their time, overlooking the pool and a pavilion in the distance. As the sun sets, enormous palm trees cast long, swaying shadows across the lawn. "Scandinavians are always looking for light," says Lars by way of explaining how Florida has become his home.

BELOW: An open-air breezeway connects the front entrance and the west garden. The wooden statues are from India.

OPPOSITE: In the hallway between the kitchen and the living room hangs a portrait of Bolander by British artist Ian Sidaway, a gift from Bolander's sons and his wife, Nadine. A bust of Swedish count Axel von Fersen, Marie Antoinette's alleged lover, sits on a French console.

ABOVE: "Bolander Beach" was accidentally created when palm trees were temporarily grouped before planting. Bolander insisted that they be left right where they were and added sand and a daybed.

OPPOSITE: The north wing contains a guest room on the ground floor and the master bedroom above. The balcony affords a view of the property.

OVERLEAF: The pool separates the main house from the pavilion. Three stone balls were found in the French countryside. The property is dotted with palm trees and boasts eighteen varieties of fruit trees.

ABOVE AND OPPOSITE: Outdoor sitting areas, including one off the main house (above), and another in the pavilion beyond the pool (opposite) reflect Lars's singular blending of disparate elements, here including Spanish sofas, Indian textiles, and rugs from Marrakech. Both spaces are hung with a rotating collection of art.

The great room attests to Bolander's ability to seamlessly mix high and low, large and small. He found two eighteenth-century Belgian wall panel paintings at the Maastricht art fair. The peapod sculptures are from a flower shop on Paris's Left Bank.

Bolander and his wife designed Bamboo Hill around the great room, where a wide-ranging collection of books, artwork, and furniture is displayed. It even includes a bronze fig tree. A circa 1800 trompe l'oeil image of a classical statue hangs in the hallway to the rear. Terra-cotta cypress tree sculptures found in Toulouse are in the foreground. French chairs are covered in one of Bolander's favorite fabrics from Rubelli. A quilted sofa from the collection of Gunter Sachs is against the wall while another sofa from Restoration Hardware anchors the room's center. Upstairs is the family's television room.

OPPOSITE: A favorite breakfast spot is a bougainvillea-covered terrace off the kitchen.

RIGHT: A painting of the famous Droste Chocolate Girl hangs next to a computer-generated portrait of Lars and Nadine by their dear friend Gunter Sachs.

FAR RIGHT AND BELOW: In the kitchen, Lars designed open shelving for cookbooks and dishes, as well as a walk-in pantry, for maximum efficiency and ease of access.

CASA AMADO

WHEN THE CURRENT OWNER OF CASA AMADO FIRST SAW the historic estate, it was in such disrepair that the visit ended not much more than a minute or two after it began. But months of touring other properties only served to convince the owner of the uniqueness of Amado's history and three-acre oceanfront setting. It is the oldest remaining Addison Mizner–designed house in Palm Beach, built in 1919 for Charles "Mr. Palm Beach" Munn. His second wife, Dorothy Spreckels Munn, lived there until 2000.

When the owner returned for another look, the place had continued to decline—most of the roof was now missing, there was evidence of surfers having partied in the house, and a rustling in the entry hall turned out to be a fox the size of a German shepherd. This time, contractor Joe Brennan came along to survey the house. With his assessment that its underlying structure was solid, what had at first seemed an unmanageable project now began to look like an opportunity.

One remaining concern was that the property was completely exposed to the neighboring house to the north, also designed by Mizner for Charlie Munn's brother Gurnee Munn, whose descendants still live there, and a grouping of six houses to the south. The owner called upon landscape architect John Lang and asked him whether, given the nature of the trees and the climate, he could provide the property with complete privacy. "He said he could, and thankfully he's a man of his word." With the assurances of both Brennan and Lang, the owner found the confidence to take on the challenge of restoring Amado to its original glory.

The owner hired Brennan's firm, Brennan Design Build, as project manager, and Brennan in turn hired Wayne Giancaterino to coordinate and direct all site work. As an opening act, Giancaterino managed to secure the building's envelope, replacing the roof, gutting the interior, and laying new floors in less than three months, thereby avoiding the costly town fees imposed on derelict buildings. Over the next few years, Giancaterino and a team of very talented local tradespeople implemented the huge quantity of drawings required to guide the renovation of the house and its grounds.

OPPOSITE: The Atlantic Ocean can be seen from almost every room of Casa Amado, designed in 1919 by Addison Mizner. It was Mizner's third commission after the Everglades Club and El Mirasol. He went on to build sixty-seven structures, establishing Palm Beach's celebrated Mediterranean Revival character.

ABOVE: Detail of the chessboard and chess pieces on the lawn.

Designer David Easton and his staff drafted most of those sketches. "Easton is not only a phenomenal decorator but is also architecturally gifted," the owner says. Pinning down Easton, who travels the world for an international clientele, was a challenge, but the effort was well worth it.

Easton remembers the first time he visited. "It was a nice house with a lot of character. But it didn't have finesse. It was a little hectic." Easton sought to meld the indoors with the outdoors to create a more relaxed flow appropriate for a vacation house. "When you're in Palm Beach, life is easier, lighter, not as formal. This is the land of beaches and sea and sunshine; you follow that and bring it into the house itself."

Easton replaced the original entrance hall, which was downstairs abutting the staff rooms on the north side of the house, with a grand, double-height hall on the west side that opens onto the living room and a dazzling view of the green lawn and sparkling ocean beyond. The owner worked closely with both Easton and his senior designer Tara Bonsignore on the décor. Together the trio created soothing interiors of soft yellows, pinks, blues, and greens.

According to Easton, "There is no great house without a great garden." Enter John Lang. "The challenge was to address the needs of a typical family and still create a classic garden feeling. I strove to create a landscape for an active, multigenerational family who like to spend their time outdoors. Our mission became to give this house another hundred years of life," says Lang. To the west of the house, Lang devised gardens that incorporate communal family activity areas, including a putting surface, a small citrus grove, a children's play area, a tennis court, and a pool. Beach views to the east were left unobstructed and simple, save for a discreet beach cabana.

Collaboration brought an iconic Palm Beach house back to life. "The specialness of the house comes from everyone who worked on it. They got everything right," says the owner. Everyone responsible for the transformation of the exteriors, interiors, and landscape—the holy trinity of house design—was passionately involved.

Thanks to the town's recent ambitious beach renourishment project, even Mother Nature is doing her bit; the beach in front of the house, which had been eroding, has been restored to its former beauty.

OPPOSITE AND ABOVE LEFT: Designer David Easton created a new, double-height entrance hall on the west side of the house.

ABOVE RIGHT: Mizner's design hallmarks include arched breezeways opening onto terraces and patios.

ABOVE: The buttery yellow of the living room walls is in elegant contrast to the deep green lawn and the blue ocean beyond. The sofas are upholstered in fabrics by Cowtan & Tout and Lee Jofa. A floral fabric by Old World Weavers enhances Louis XVI–style bergères.

TOP, CENTER, AND BOTTOM RIGHT: Family antiques, including a red chinoiserie secretary, add character and complexity to the living room.

OVERLEAF LEFT: An elegantly arched hallway frames a view of the dining room.

OVERLEAF RIGHT: The dining room's original dark stone floor was replaced with blond wood. Hand-painted, whimsical chinoiserie wallpaper by Gracie brightens up the room. The chairs are Italian Rococo in style. The consoles were custom made by Frederick P. Victoria & Son.

OPPOSITE, TOP LEFT, AND TOP RIGHT: In the master bedroom, which overlooks the ocean, a cheerful Lee Jofa floral pattern is used for the wallpaper, bed hangings, and curtains. A 1790 Piedmontese chandelier from Scott Barnes Antiques hangs from the center of the ceiling. The carpet is by Patterson Flynn Martin.

ABOVE: Elegant paneling lends this bathroom the atmosphere of a clubby retreat.

OVERLEAF: The family room opens onto shaded terraces overlooking the gardens and the ocean beyond, blending indoor and outdoor living. The curtain fabric is from Lee Jofa and the iron chandelier, reminiscent of a Mizner design, is by Formations.

ABOVE AND OPPOSITE: Casa Amado's restored oceanfront façade is classic Mizner, incorporating arched loggias, tile roofs, turrets and towers, courtyards, and stone fountains.

OVERLEAF LEFT: Three overgrown oceanfront acres were reimagined by Lang Design Group Landscape Architects. A stone fountain is the focal point of a garden between the main house and the tennis pavilion.

OVERLEAF RIGHT: A second-floor terrace provides a view of a courtyard, the pool, and the tennis court pavilion beyond.

PRECEDING PAGES: The pool is long enough for swimming laps; tucked into its sides are shallow children's play areas. The area is bordered with hedges and trelliswork swathed in fragrant jasmine.

ABOVE AND OPPOSITE: Outdoor amenities are positioned close to one another so members of the multigenerational family can enjoy different activities at the same time. A comfortable tennis pavilion and cabana, situated between the pool and tennis courts, enables the pool and tennis courts to be viewed simultaneously. The structure is also used for al fresco dining. An outdoor chessboard was created in a shaded area of the lawn.

PASSION PLAY

FOR YEARS, DESIGNERS, ARTISTS, AND MEDIA ORGANIzations have been putting down stakes in Palm Beach County. They're drawn by the locale's proximity to an international airport, luminous days, and burgeoning literary, art, and film scene—anchored by the Society of the Four Arts, the Norton Gallery of Art, and the Palm Beach International Film Festival. Art patron Beth Rudin DeWoody grew up visiting Palm Beach with her parents but eventually found her comfort zone in the hipper purlieu of West Palm Beach's historic Northwood section. "When I was young, my family had a house on Eden Road. We spent our days at the Palm Beach Country Club. My big thrill was looking out of the cabana and seeing John F. Kennedy teeing off."

DeWoody and her siblings continued visiting her parents with their own growing families in tow. One morning she woke up to find her son sleeping on a chaise longue, having been beaten to the last bed by a cousin. "It was time to find a place of our own. I wanted something on the water, but prices in Palm Beach were prohibitive." DeWoody put her famous instinct for identifying and nurturing up-and-coming artists to work when choosing a property. "I've always loved neighborhoods on the verge. I lived in Tribeca in the '70s, and I've been in Southampton since 1975, eventually buying a place in the Art Village neighborhood in 1979. Northwood was creating a historic district, closing off streets with planted roundabouts, and nearby Citiplace and Clematis Street had just been redone," DeWoody recalls, referring to a new shopping development and the revitalization of a historic street in downtown West Palm Beach.

DeWoody purchased a house and an attached empty lot to the north that looked directly across the Intracoastal at the Palm Beach Country Club golf course of her childhood days. Eventually, she purchased a neighboring cottage, passing along her original house to her two grown children and thereby creating a family compound. A devotee of Modernism, DeWoody suspected her cottage had architectural merit and discovered that it had been designed in the 1950s by Florida's "Master of the S curve," the architect Howard Chilton. According to the *Palm Beach Daily News*, Chilton cited

OPPOSITE: Sylvie Fleury's giant mushroom welcomes visitors to art patron Beth DeWoody's Modernist house. Sculptures by Tony Rosenthal greet guests on the front porch.

ABOVE: Robert Indiana's *Love* sculpture is one of many works of art that enliven DeWoody's dining room.

the Greek amphitheater as his inspiration and aspired to "capture all of nature's gifts" with his airy designs, which can still be seen in sinuous apartment buildings along Palm Beach's South Lake Drive and North Ocean Boulevard.

DeWoody went about sprucing up the place to accommodate her growing art collection. "The furniture, walls, and rugs are neutral so the art takes center stage," she says of her design scheme.

DeWoody's bounteous art collection includes works by Sylvie Fleury, Claude Lalanne, Robert Indiana, and a shimmering silver bicycle by the Belgian duo Amaral-Bostyn, which hangs over the living room fireplace, all testifying to Beth's wide-ranging and eclectic taste. About positioning her art, she says, "There are no hard-and-fast rules; everything is done by eye. I just try to make a relationship between the pieces."

DeWoody scoured nearby Dixie Highway for Postmodern furniture. A well-known dealers' mea culpa became, "We're low on inventory. Beth was just here." Everyone knew they were referring to Beth DeWoody.

DeWoody's friends are as wide ranging and plentiful as her art collection, and she loves sharing her home and its treasures with them. To that end, she commissioned architect Hugh Huddleson to build an outdoor bar and barbecue, complete with changing rooms and showers. For parties, she parks a vintage Airstream, transformed by artist Randy Polumbo into *Lovestream*, on the grass. With its jaw-dropping art collection and view of the sparkling Intracoastal beyond, DeWoody's West Palm Beach residence never fails to give her guests a visual thrill.

ABOVE: A Buddha head by Noh Sang-Kyoon, from his *For the Worshipers* series, 2001.

BELOW: An iconic sheep by Claude Lalanne guards the entrance hall. The brass sculpture at left is by Harry Bertoia.

OPPOSITE: A delicate Peter Coffin sculpture graces the entrance hall. DeWoody added beams to the living room ceiling.

OVERLEAF: The eyes have it. A pair of eyes by Liz Craft overlooks the living room, observed by another eye sculpture by Tim Hawkinson. A work by Postconceptualist Warren Neidich hangs over a sculpture by Isamu Noguchi. An ink drawing on paper by Debra Hampton has pride of place in this area of the living room. The stairs lead to the master bedroom.

PRECEDING PAGES: The dining room is filled with contemporary works: the vase on the pedestal is by Erwin Wurm; the noose is by Liza Lou; the shopping bag is by Sylvie Fleury; the *Love* sculpture is by Robert Indiana; the drum is by Bruce Conner; and the white lid is by Richard Haden.

TOP LEFT AND RIGHT: A collection of Blenko glass brightens a shelf in the living room.

ABOVE: The entrance to the library is flanked by a Heinz Mack work to the left and a metal fly by Rob Wynne to the right. In the left foreground is a sectional work by Jim Lambie.

OPPOSITE: A bicycle sculpture by Amaral-Bostyn hangs over the fireplace. The floor lamps are by Tommi Parzinger.

PRECEDING PAGES: View of the Palm Beach Country Club golf course across the Intracoastal. Sculptures dotting the lawn include, clockwise from center, a shark by Claude Lalanne, a dandelion sculpture by Paul Morrison, three cans by Iran do Espírito Santo, and an *Endless Column* (after Brancusi) by Richard Pettibone.

OPPOSITE, ABOVE, AND OVERLEAF: The interior of an Airstream was transformed by artist Randy Polumbo into *Lovestream*. It is parked on the lawn for parties.

OPPOSITE: Sylvie Fleury's
iridescent giant mushroom.

ABOVE: A picnic table by
Vincent Mazeau drips with
glowing icicles.

TOP LEFT: Rob Wynne's mirrored-glass sculpture *Almost Nothing* is mounted above the bed in the master bedroom.

TOP RIGHT: Timothy Horn's fancifully decorative *Galatea*, based on an eighteenth-century earring pattern, hangs above a Pedro Friedeberg Hand Chair.

ABOVE: The pecky cypress ceiling and beams lend a tropical note to the room.

OPPOSITE: Beneath a work by John M. Armleder is a table from Grosfeld House, on which are displayed a bust by Rob Wynne and a plastic case by American sculptor Ernest Trova.

VILLA ARTEMIS

IN PALM BEACH, THE METICULOUS OVERHAUL OF A HIStoric mansion is hardly a curiosity. But there is nothing typical about the reincarnation of an iconic house that has been in the same family for more than fifty years. Villa Artemis remains one of the last vestiges of a bygone era, when quiet elegance was the order of the day. "When I was growing up, even family lunches were formal. It's how my mother liked things. I would have much rather been by the pool with a reflector," says Jane Rosenthal Horvitz, recalling holidays spent in the house her father purchased as a retreat from frigid Ohio winters. Jane and her husband, Michael, continue to convene here with their own family, though weekends are more relaxed than those of her childhood. "We do puzzles, play tennis, and gather by the pool. Our children bring lots of friends. We wanted the house to accommodate a more modern lifestyle."

Built in 1916, Villa Artemis's Regency design was a departure for architect F. Burrall Hoffman, whose most famous work was Miami's Mediterranean Revival masterpiece, Villa Vizcaya. When Jane Horvitz's father, the late Leighton Rosenthal, purchased the house in 1959 as a surprise for his wife, Honey, he enlisted Palm Beach architect Marion Sims Wyeth to remove the second floor and enclose an interior courtyard to create a new living room. The modifications streamlined the house to make it more manageable and a less obtrusive presence in the surrounding landscape. Jane and Michael Horvitz sought to continue this approach when bringing the property into the twenty-first century.

"We wanted to be realistic about how we use the house," Michael Horvitz says. "We spend days in the pool house so we enhanced that, giving it a nicer living room, guest rooms, and kitchen. The downstairs of the main house was a warren of storage rooms, so we turned those into guest rooms."

They called upon Mark Ferguson of the New York architectural firm Ferguson & Shamamian, with whom they had worked on three other projects. "They were intent

OPPOSITE: The living room's subtle color scheme befits both the warm climate and the restrained architecture. The doorway was widened to expand the view.

ABOVE: Detail of the fireplace surround in the living room. Although added in the early 1960s during a major modification of the house, the classical head typifies Regency design, which became popular in Palm Beach following the building of Villa Artemis in 1916.

on not changing the house," Ferguson recalls, "but they wanted it more open to the daylight, more porous to the outdoors."

Narrow accesses on either side of the living room were expanded, giving the room the feeling of a breezeway between the dining room and the sunroom, and affording sweeping views of the enormous pool and the Atlantic to the east and a tennis court and rose garden to the west. The most significant addition was a house for Jane Horvitz's sister, Cynthia Boardman. Michael Horvitz and Ferguson sited it to the southeast of the main house, directly across the from pool house, augmenting the symmetry and elegance typical of Regency design.

When it came to the interiors, Jane Horvitz "wanted to keep everything very clean and breezy and incorporate some of the furniture we already had." They hired interior designer David Kleinberg, who says, "It's a family house in the truest sense of the word. Jane lived here as a child and as a young bride; she has raised her own children here; and now her children bring their grown friends. She wanted it refreshed, but she didn't want to toss everything out."

Simultaneously, the family asked Mario Nievera to help with the landscape design. Nievera proposed introducing horticulture that wasn't available fifty years ago and adding subtle splashes of color that would bring attention to the elegant simplicity of the house's façade. St. Augustine grass was replaced with zoysia grass, which withstands the saltwater spray. Restrained groupings of confederate jasmine, white hibiscus, and purple bougainvillea provide accents. "It was all about integrating a modern family into a house while paying homage to the history of the house and their memories of it," Nievera says. The Preservation Foundation of Palm Beach recognized Nievera, the Horvitzes, and Cynthia Boardman with the annual Lesly S. Smith Landscape Award.

Jane Horvitz is pleased with the outcome. "I didn't want anything overdone; rather, we wanted to bring it up-to-date and make it more livable." This incarnation should last another fifty years.

OPPOSITE: White hibiscus and purple bougainvillea were introduced to add subtle splashes of color to the façade. The original pale turquoise trim was retained.

BELOW: Situating the new house to the southeast of the main house created an elegant entrance courtyard. Vines soften the façade of the new building.

TOP: Barware commemorates cities of note.

ABOVE: Villa Artemis was awarded the Palm Beach Preservation Foundation's Lesly S. Smith Landscape Award.

RIGHT: The living room was created in the early 1960s by enclosing an open-air courtyard. The moldings are original to the house, but the fireplace mantel and surround were added at that time. The painting over the mantel is by Saul Chase. Energy-efficient skylights bathe the room in natural light. The sofas are covered in appliquéd damask.

LEFT: A palette of blues and blue-greens creates a fresh, breezy guest room. Palm trees planted outside the window enhance the tropical feel.

BELOW left: Roses from the garden perfume the room.

BELOW right: A photograph by the owner of the house, Jane Horvitz, hangs above the fireplace.

OPPOSITE: Coral orange imparts a cozy—and tropical—atmosphere to the library. White upholstery and brushed-copper furnishings keep it brisk. A painting by Hans Hofmann hangs between the windows.

ABOVE: The color scheme in the master bedroom is a soothing combination of blues and white.

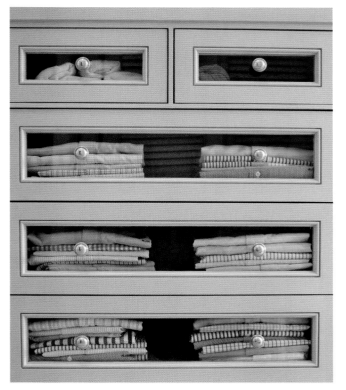

TOP RIGHT: A charming watercolor of Villa Artemis by John S. Coles rests among family photographs and vacation keepsakes.

ABOVE RIGHT: The owner's neatly stacked shirts are easily viewed through glass-fronted drawers.

OVERLEAF: A sunroom separates the upper terrace from the living room. The black cast-iron urns and sphinx sculptures are original to the house. A crisp black-and-white awning shades the pool house.

PAGE 170: The owners replaced the temple's original bronze sculpture of Artemis with a marble version.

PAGE 171: The black cast-iron sculptures and urns are typical of neoclassical design.

OPPOSITE TOP AND BOTTOM: The family spends most of their time in the pool house, which was updated with a new kitchen, family room, and guest rooms. Indoor/outdoor terry cloth pillows add color.

TOP LEFT: Friezes above the windows lend elegance to the neoclassical design. Narrow terraces, edged in hibiscus and boxwood, were created outside the ground-floor guest rooms

TOP RIGHT: A table on the western terrace, overlooking the tennis court and rose garden, is set for breakfast.

ABOVE LEFT: A typical breakfast setting.

ABOVE RIGHT: A mermaid sculpture presides over the formal rose garden.

ST. LUCIE RANCH

JORGE SÁNCHEZ, ALONG WITH BUSINESS PARTNER PHIL Maddux, is the gardening mastermind behind many of Palm Beach's most admired private and public spaces, including the celebrated greening of iconic Worth Avenue. He prepared for the job growing radishes in his native Cuba as a young boy and working on his family's Martin County sugar-cane farm after immigrating to Florida as a teenager.

Countless commercial triumphs enabled Sánchez to indulge in a personal project on a scope that would have intimidated even the most assured horticulturist. Every weekend Sánchez swaps his drafting table for a backhoe and heads for the vast outreaches of the county, where he and his wife, Serina, purchased 640 acres of scrubland. "I got to know this area by driving to and fro from my family's sugar-cane farm. It always captivated me. I thought if I could ever design a place of my own, I'd like it to be here."

Sánchez estimated that it would take at least ten years for the property of pine stands, oak hammocks, and palmetto flats to attain the form he imagined. "My wife and I bought it as an investment and as a place where we could spend the rest of our lives bettering the land," Sánchez says. With the help of the Nature Conservancy, Sánchez started thinning the woods, chopping palmettos and getting rid of the exotics.

After a year of analyzing airflow and scenic views, he and Serina chose the northern section of the property on which to build a charming tin-roofed cabin to be used as a weekend retreat. Nearby, he dug a five-acre spring-fed lake. Later came stables, a manager's house, a workshop, and a machine shed.

More recently, the couple made "a small improvement," says Jorge, whose clients uniformly describe him as courtly and understated. This "small improvement" is a 10,000-square-foot, one-bedroom folly that rises out of the flat plain like a whale surfacing. Named the Warehouse, the residence was conceptually intended to serve as a "storage space" for antiques garnered from Serina's childhood home on Long Island,

OPPOSITE: Serina and Jorge Sánchez named their ranch St. Lucie in honor of both Santa Lucia, as the Sánchez family sugar mill in Cuba was called, and Port St. Lucie, where the Sánchezes' sugar-cane farm in Florida was located.

ABOVE: Detail of the tile floor on the porch off the dining room. Often referred to as Cuban tile, it is very similar to that on the veranda of the Administration House, an old sugar mill in central Cuba.

Knole, a famous estate designed by Thomas Hastings of the renowned firm Carrère & Hastings, the architects of the New York Public Library.

Now the focal point of the Sánchezes' St. Lucie Ranch, the Warehouse was designed by Miami architects Rafael Portuondo and Jose Luis Gonzalez-Perotti. It blends elements of Serina's formal childhood home and the tropical houses of Jorges's Cuban heritage, most notably a dramatic parapet.

Guests are reminded of the hosts' combined heritage when served a lunch of rice, beans, and pork presented in covered silver tureens etched with Serina's family crest. The afternoon might include a game of bridge, fishing, or a swim in the enormous circular pool. Most visitors opt for a drive around the property, where Jorge is experimenting with tropical hybrids of sycamores, not known to do well in this area, as well as silk floss, kapoks, and water oaks. An organic garden features olive, mulberry, fig, pomegranate, and apple trees. A sabal palm allée reflects Jorge's installation at the New York Botanical Garden, where he was also commissioned to create the exhibitions *The Orchid Show: Cuba in Flower* and *Wild Medicine: Healing Plants Around the World, Featuring the Italian Renaissance Garden.*

Jorge and Serina view the vast, grassy landscape, still predominantly in its natural state, as equity for their children and grandchildren, who are already enjoying their inheritance by visiting on weekends. The couple's son is currently initiating a grass-raised beef operation, but thus far, no radish beds.

BELOW: The entrance gate and post were designed by the ranch's owner, landscape architect Jorge Sánchez. The posts are "snags," naturally dried native slash pines.

OPPOSITE: Sculpted from repurposed slash pines, the stumpery serves as a natural entrance to the camellia and azalea garden, where the family dog, Blackie, often retreats in search of shade.

OVERLEAF LEFT: The house, designed by Portuondo Perotti Architects, was done in the style of eighteenth-century Cuban architecture and incorporates details from Sánchez family houses in Cuba, including a dramatic parapet.

OVERLEAF RIGHT: A porch off the master bedroom provides a constant breeze and sweeping views of the vast property.

PRECEDING PAGES LEFT: The dimensions of the entrance hall in the Warehouse are similar to those in Serina's childhood home, Knole, a Long Island estate designed by Thomas Hastings. The George Brookshaw polychrome-painted and parcel-gilt console was positioned in a similar location at Knole. The black-and-white tile floor is reminiscent of the floor in Jorge's maternal grandparents' house in Havana.

PRECEDING PAGES RIGHT: Curved staircases on either side of the entrance hall lead up to the main landing, where the public rooms are found.

OPPOSITE: The sculpted living room entrance was inspired by Jorge's eighteenth-century family house in Havana. The antique twig planter is one of four that grace each side of the landing.

ABOVE: The Warehouse was conceived to accommodate furniture that Serina Sánchez inherited from her family house, including a William Kent side table and pictures of the Phipps family taken by Tony Soluri for *Town & Country*.

FAR LEFT, LEFT, AND OPPOSITE: A refectory table from the South Hall at Knole serves as the dining room table. The chairs, side tables, and flower containers were crafted from trees on the Knole property by an artisan in Oyster Bay, New York. An old carpet found in the estate's basement was used to cover the chair seats. The sofa is from Serina's childhood bedroom. The antlers above the doors were dropped by local deer.

ABOVE: Antique fishing rods are stored in a wooden box marked with Serina's father's name, Esmond Bradley Martin. The record-breaking salmon Martin caught in 1943 hangs over the mantel.

ABOVE: The overdoor paintings, depicting Jorge and Serina riding at the ranch, are by Raoul de Sibour.

OPPOSITE: The family spends most of their time on the outdoor porch, which is off the dining room. A floor of colorful Cuban cement tiles is cool underfoot.

ABOVE: An octagonal kitchen provides views of the property's approach, lake, barns, and paddocks. During the winter, orchids are brought inside to protect them from frost.

In the master bedroom, a George III side chair and a pencil drawing of Bradley Martin, Serina's uncle, as a child are next to a George III cabinet featuring satinwood and tulipwood inlay and an inset reverse-painted mirror.

The canopy bed belonged to Serina's parents. In a bold design move, Serina swathed the entire room in a floral-print fabric.

OPPOSITE: A sunroom off of the bedroom is a favorite spot for this family of avid bridge players.

Hidden by woodlands, the swimming pool is equidistant from the property's tin-roofed cabin and the Warehouse. *Elaeocarpus* and bleached live oaks provide shade. The pool's circular shape ensures that no one area has design prominence. The stone fruit baskets once decorated Knole's garden courtyard. The red furniture adds visual interest.

OPPOSITE: In 2000, Jorge and Serina Sánchez purchased 640 acres northwest of Palm Beach in neighboring Martin County and set about restoring the land to its natural beauty. Now the St. Lucie Ranch incorporates barns, numerous gardens, and a five-acre spring-fed lake, where the family enjoys fishing, canoeing, and picnicking. The sculpture (bottom right) is an eighteenth-century Italian marble figure depicting Autumn. It was the centerpiece of Knole's topiary garden.

ABOVE: At St. Lucie Ranch, Palm Beachers Serina and Jorge Sánchez trade in bikes for horses. The Warehouse can be seen through the stable window.

HAUTE BOHEMIAN

KATHARINE "KATHY" AND WILLIAM "BILLY" RAYNER's Palm Beach house reflects their easy elegance. Exotic furnishings, dazzling antique textiles, and stucco walls in vibrant colors seemingly blended in a spice market establish a global theme. Scattered memorabilia and watercolors by Billy Rayner, depicting scenes of Near Eastern and North African travels suggest the interiors are a work in progress. It's hard to believe that this intriguing residence and its alluring gardens originated as a nondescript ranch with good proportions. "My husband, Billy, grew up in Palm Beach. We purchased this small house so we'd have an escape to walk the dogs and go to movies."

Soon after acquiring the property, Kathy Rayner contacted architect Peter Marino. Marino and Rayner had been friends before he received his big break—the commission to design Andy Warhol's New York townhouse in the 1970s. "Peter was rather square back then. He wore a bow tie," Rayner says of the architect, who is as well known for his Mohawk and edgy biker garb as he is for conceiving boutiques that articulate the image of upscale brands—Chanel, Dior, and Louis Vuitton, among many others.

"Peter can do anything. He has a phenomenal eye for detail. He visualizes most things in his head. He just hooks on to one fact about a client and goes from there," says Rayner.

In this instance, Marino took his cue from the Rayners' wanderlust. "Kathy and Billy travel everywhere in the world and have a wonderful sense of the exotic," Marino observes. The Palm Beach home, he notes, is specifically a "reflection of their appreciation of Ottoman-inspired and Moroccan-crafted architecture."

They painted the living room walls tangerine. "I love orange walls. Art looks very good against it," says Rayner. Orientalist-style banquettes, bespoke furniture, and casement windows were commissioned. The walls of a tiny library were paneled, painted white, and stenciled. Marino lengthened the existing pool and centered it on the French doors of the master bedroom.

Though the main house remains a modest one-bedroom, the property was transformed into the intimate escape originally envisioned. Tiny guesthouses resembling

OPPOSITE: One of the residence's two pools fronts the Turkish pavilion. It is rimmed with a stone walkway punctuated by pots of the owner's beloved roses. The junglelike garden beyond is shaded with towering royal palms.

ABOVE: A detail of the hand stenciling on the wall of a guest room in the Turkish pavilion.

potting sheds are hidden in the lush landscape, their entries accessed via narrow paved paths, providing privacy and an element of jungle exoticism.

Inspired by gardens far and near, including the Majorelle Garden in Marrakech, the "jungle" surrounding the late Lilly Pulitzer's house, and the Ann Norton Sculpture Garden in West Palm Beach, the Rayners asked garden designer Denis Lamarsh to create the property's lush, tropical envelope. Neighbors offered towering royal palms that had grown too immense for their own gardens.

Eventually, the Rayners purchased an adjoining lot on which a Turkish pavilion, inspired by Billy Rayner's sketches of the Topkapi Palace in Istanbul, was built. The pavilion comprises an entertainment area flanked by two guest rooms. "By pavilion-izing the structures, one never feels crowded; privacy reigns; bedrooms are divided among three buildings," explains Marino.

To frame the Turkish pavilion, Kathy Rayner asked gardener Michael Peasley to create a Persian-style garden, including coquina fountains, a blue reflecting pool, potted roses, silver date palms, and Chinese evergreens. The Preservation Foundation of Palm Beach awarded the property the prestigious Lesly S. Smith Landscape Award.

As the Rayners continue to travel and accumulate design ideas, the house constantly evolves, while retaining its focus as a personal retreat. "It's really a separate world for Billy and me," Kathy says. "You forget where you are when you're here."

RIGHT: A Moorish-style fountain covered in floral-patterned, multicolored tiles sets a Moroccan mood in the entrance courtyard of the Rayners' house, designed by Peter Marino and inspired by the owners' travels to North Africa and the Near East.

ABOVE: A pathway of ceramic tiles snakes through a tropical jungle to the entrance gate. The cobalt blue of the wall lining the path and the exterior of the main house is reminiscent of the predominant color of Yves Saint Laurent's Majorelle Garden in Marrakech.

The walls of William Rayner's small library in the main house are paneled, whitewashed, and stenciled.

In keeping with the home's Moroccan spirit, Kathy Rayner choose to paint the drawing room a deep tangerine.

OVERLEAF LEFT: Annie, the
family's beloved Labrador,
sits by the Moroccan-inspired
"Camel" pool. Curved coconut
palm trees provide shade.

OVERLEAF RIGHT: The master
bedroom overlooks the
Camel pool.

PRECEDING PAGES AND OPPOSITE: An outdoor Moroccan-style dining tent, permanently pitched near the Camel pool, is the Rayners' favorite dinner spot. The deep green tropical foliage sets off the vivid blue banquette and chairs. The blue is achieved by mixing purple into the paint.

ABOVE: The floral arrangement is by Tom Mathieu of Worth Avenue.

RIGHT: The tablecloth is in the North African style.

BELOW: A mirror in the dining tent reflects the nearby pool.

Carved wooden furniture and gilt-framed mirrors decorate the Turkish pavilion.

ABOVE: Cozy banquettes lining either side of the pavilion's main room provide maximum seating.

OPPOSITE: A riot of vibrant fabrics and stenciling covers the walls, ceiling, and furnishings in the fantastical Turkish pavilion, inspired by Billy Rayner's sketches of Istanbul's Topkapi Palace and designed by architect Peter Marino. The intricately carved wooden doorways open onto an enchanting Persian-style garden.

OPPOSITE, ABOVE, AND OVERLEAF: Guest rooms flank the Turkish pavilion's central room and overlook a pool paved with stone in a pattern conceived by the owner. Beneath its domed ceiling, the interior of this guest room is a heady mix of patterns in blues, pinks, reds, gold, and oranges.

PRECEDING PAGES: A floral-patterned, multicolored tile fireplace surround, a hallmark of Arabic design, anchors the main room of the Turkish pavilion. Through the ornate, hand-carved wooden doors can be seen the fountains and stenciled orange walls of the Persian-style garden, planted with wart ferns and two enormous *Phoenix sylvestris* (silver date) palms, which create a cathedral effect.

ABOVE AND OPPOSITE: A striking aqua soffit offsets the pavilion's exterior walls, which are painted deep orange and hand stenciled with Persian motifs.

LEFT: Leafy palms, a tile floor, rich orange walls stenciled in blue, and a trickling stone fountain, impart an exotic tone to the intimate garden, which incorporates typical Persian hallmarks, including scent, symmetry, and subdued plant colors.

BELOW: Stonework by Schatzi McLean surrounds two fountains in the Persian-inspired garden.

OVERLEAF: An eight-pointed star fashioned of Moroccan tile is the centerpiece of a courtyard paved with coquina stone and custom Uzbek tiles that echo the colors of a small guesthouse and its ornately carved and painted wooden door.

APARTMENTS

PALM BEACH'S PROXIMITY TO AN INTERNATIONAL AIR-port has made apartment living fashionable for those who crave a turnkey seasonal or weekend getaway. It's been said that the true measure of a designer's inventiveness should be judged not by his or her ability to create a modern masterpiece or conceive a residence from scratch, but rather, by his or her capacity to transform a nondescript box into a warm, functional living space. The apartments presented on the following pages demonstrate that limited floor space and stringent architectural codes can be a challenging testing ground for ingenious interior décor. These heirloom dwellings are tucked into desirable, conveniently positioned Palm Beach locations, including a serpentine building overlooking Lake Worth and a romantic apartment house towering over historic Worth Avenue.

EAST-MEETS-WEST ESCAPE

When Manila-born designer Josie Natori and her husband, Ken, were seeking a warm escape with easy access to and from New York, she fell hard for a lakefront Palm Beach apartment with a spacious terrace that provided a view of bobbing yachts filtered through a curtain of rustling palm trees. "It reminded me of Manila, my hometown," Natori says.

Predictably, Natori transformed the interiors to reflect her international lifestyle. "It's the East-meets-West design aesthetic—contemporary sofas surrounded by antiquities. It's simple but sophisticated." The Natoris commissioned Calvin Tsao, of the New York firm Tsao & McKown Architects, who had designed five personal and commercial spaces for the Natoris and had an innate sense of their needs, to design the interior. Tsao increased the sense of space by blurring the distinction between indoors and outdoors. For instance, he repeated design elements such as matching end tables both

OPPOSITE: Mahogany shutters were installed on the terrace to provide relief from the afternoon sun and to frame the view of bobbing boats moored at the nearby dock. The pendant lights are by Property. The cushions are from Walker Zabriskie in nearby Via Parigi.

ABOVE: Detail of the geometrically patterned railing on the terrace. The apartment building was designed by Howard Chilton in 1961 in his signature serpentine style.

on the terrace and in the adjacent living/dining area. The lantern over the dining room table echoes the geometric pattern in the terrace railing. Sliding glass doors edged in thick mahogany serve to frame the view. A piano is a dominant element in every Natori residence—at the age of nine she first performed with the Manila Philharmonic Orchestra.

The tranquil retreat is exactly what the couple envisioned. Their boat is anchored at the dock, the amenity that initially attracted the designer to the apartment. When in residence, her husband fishes and plays golf, but for Natori, "Palm Beach is a place to recharge . . . to do absolutely nothing—sit by the pool, read, and spend time in the sun. And of course, play my piano!"

BELOW: The dining area is painted off-white and hung with a geometric lantern that echoes the pattern of the terrace railing. The guest room beyond serves as a study and music room. The pairing of a painting by Ross Bleckner (not seen in the photo) and an Indonesian textile draped over the custom-made daybed is indicative of Natori's penchant for East-meets-West design.

OPPOSITE: A sparkling mixed-media work by Brooklyn artist Auguste Garufi dominates the living room and reflects the sunlight. Architect Calvin Tsao designed the sofa, chairs, ottoman, and carpet. The cheerfully patterned pillows are from the Josie Natori Collection.

In the master bedroom,
Tsao attached a 1940s reading
lamp to a custom-designed
headboard.

ABOVE: The coverlet, embroidered pillows, and throw are by Natori Bedding.

BELOW LEFT: A silver-and-shell sculpture rests on the desk.

ABOVE LEFT: The vibrant orange chair and ottoman in the bedroom add punch to the apartment's otherwise neutral tones.

ABOVE RIGHT: The vintage desk is by Sergio Rodrigues; the lamp, from Blackman Cruz.

HIGH-OCTANE VINTAGE

Interior designer Meg Braff's West Palm Beach apartment features brilliant sherbet colors that reflect her warmth and infectious zest for life. "In Florida, I use bright colors. Anything else can get lost," says Braff. The Mississippi native has an antiques shop in Locust Valley, New York, which also serves as headquarters for the production of her eponymous fabric, wallpaper, and furniture lines, as well as the management of design jobs from Newport to Jamaica.

Braff first purchased the apartment not only to establish a professional presence in the area but also to provide a retreat in which to hunker down and work. From there she scouts vintage items in stores clustered on nearby Dixie Highway and the neighborhood called Northwood by locals.

Eventually, Braff annexed the apartment next door, turning the space into a three-bedroom getaway for her family. Now Meg, her husband, and four sons with varying school and sports schedules rotate through the apartment all winter, often leaving the key behind for Braff's parents. In keeping with the apartment's original intent, Braff transformed a fourth bedroom into an office sanctuary. Even when the apartment is full of family, she has a private space in which to revitalize her creative flow, scanning design books and magazines while her husband and boys hit the beach.

BELOW: The simple lines of a white Billy Baldwin sofa are the perfect counterpoint to the brightly colored stripes of the cotton rug. A floor-to-ceiling mirror reflects the view of Lake Worth.

OPPOSITE: The dining room's orange and yellow scheme takes its cue from the adjoining living room and terrace, where sunlight pours in all day long. The table and chairs were found along Dixie Highway.

OVERLEAF LEFT: In the guest bedroom (top left) and the boys' bedroom (top right), structural white vintage furnishings are set off by brilliant blues. In contrast, the master bedroom (bottom left and right) is pink. "I have a lot of boys in my life. I deserve a pink bedroom," says Braff.

OVERLEAF RIGHT: Streamlined furnishings and a Lucite coffee table enable the buoyant aqua and orange wallpaper to take center stage in Braff's office hideaway.

STATE OF GRACE

A bust of the wife's father wears a hat that once belonged to Tom Mix, star of many early Westerns.

In the spring of 1918, Paris Singer, heir to the Singer sewing machine fortune, visited Palm Beach with noted society architect Addison Mizner in tow. Seduced by the island's balmy climate and inspired by the prevailing war effort, Singer and Mizner set out to build a convalescent home for soldiers at the far west end of Worth Avenue. Armistice Day arrived long before the building's completion, motivating Singer and Mizner to revise their plans and create a private club. The Everglades Club opened on January 25, 1919, exposing islanders to Mizner's architectural sleight of hand and forever altering the face of Palm Beach. The club's Moorish towers and fanciful courtyards appealed immensely to the members, many of whom commissioned houses in a similar style, thus launching Palm Beach's Mediterranean Revival building craze, which continues to this day.

A stretch of shops to the east and west of the Everglades Club, developed by Singer and designed by Mizner, became the forerunner of today's Worth Avenue, which, with the series of intimate arcades radiating out from it, is considered one of the world's most alluring shopping streets. Ada Louise Huxtable, a former architecture critic for the *New York Times*, called Mizner's shopping arcades "a superb act of theater and urban design."

Above these arcades, or vias, Mizner and Singer created vast, fanciful apartments, many with stained-glass windows and towers, most of which remain private residences that rarely change hands. When a longtime Palm Beach couple heard that an apartment might become available, they went to see it and were immediately entranced by the 360-degree views. Moreover, creaky wood floors and faded painted ceilings aligned perfectly with their aesthetic.

Mizner famously preferred everything "chipped, cracked and busted," going so far as to maintain a workshop in West Palm Beach where wood beams were distressed by scraping them with broken bottles, and furniture was drilled to simulate wormholes. Though the couple came by the patina on their belongings a bit more honestly, almost everything they owned was also perfectly imperfect. The wife inherited pieces, including old master paintings, from a childhood home designed by Mrs. Drury McMillen and a farm in Ireland where her father bred racehorses. She claims to have spent more than she earned during her tenure as a print expert at Christie's auction house. The husband had enough family trophies to make Ralph Lauren, whose shop is below, weep with envy.

A tiny passenger elevator meant that their belongings had to be hoisted through a window by crane. "We're never leaving. We can't!" says the wife happily. The inconvenience quickly diminished the first time the couple took a front row seat for the bright orange sunset that illuminated the red barrel-tiled roofs below and the Intracoastal Waterway before disappearing behind West Palm Beach's growing skyline.

OPPOSITE: An old master painting is perfectly at home in a living room designed in the 1920s by Addison Mizner, whose work was famously inspired by Romanesque, Gothic, and Renaissance architecture.

OVERLEAF: Hand-painted beams, designed by Mizner, decorate the living room ceiling. Prince of Wales–style chairs surround the dining room table. The window is flanked by a seventeenth-century Venetian painting on the left and a seventeenth-century Dutch oil on the right.

LEFT: In the master bedroom, an ancestral drum table is flanked by vintage chairs found at an antiques shop on West Palm Beach's Dixie Highway. The wife, a former print specialist at Christie's, collects botanicals.

BELOW: A writing desk that once belonged to the husband's parents.

REGENCY REJUVENATED

Swiss-born American architect Maurice Fatio's charm extended beyond his majestic 1920s Mediterranean Revival houses; an impeccable dresser, he was also famous for his mastery of the tango. His homes were so sought after, his personality so alluring, that Cole Porter wrote in a song, "I want to live on Maurice Fatio's patio."

After arriving in New York in 1920, Fatio formed a partnership with William A. Treanor and eventually followed his social clients south, opening a satellite office in Palm Beach in 1925 at the young age of twenty-eight. Commissions immediately besieged him, including the Mediterranean Revival mansion Il Palmetto, a 40,000-square-foot ocean-to-lake estate for Philadelphia industrialist Joseph Widener. Once owned by magazine heiress Janet Annenberg Hooker, it was purchased in 1999 by Netscape cofounder James H. Clark. Whether designed in the Mediterranean Revival, Georgian Revival, French Norman, British Colonial, Regency Revival, or contemporary style, Fatio's houses were prized for their beautiful entrances, high ceilings, symmetry, and balanced proportions.

When a Fatio Regency Revival house became available, Diahann Cochran thought it was grander than she and her husband, Jay, needed. But its many assets were alluring enough to convince the young couple that they could recast it into the snug family home they craved. Located on a quiet street between Palm Beach's Southern Estate section and Worth Avenue, it was within walking distance of both the center of town and the beach. An outbuilding had a small apartment for houseguests, and its large garage was accessed from a driveway at the back of the house, allowing Jay, an endurance sports-car driver whose career highlights include winning Daytona's Rolex 24 and racing for the Dyson team, to come and go discreetly when taking his beloved cars and motorcycles for spins.

The couple turned to local architect Jeff Smith. Smith has the blueprint of every historical house in Palm Beach stamped on his memory and the deft ability to reimagine them for modern, gracious living.

OPPOSITE: Two forty-foot-tall Cuban mahogany trees frame the entrance of this Regency Revival house designed by Maurice Fatio.

ABOVE: Beads are an African souvenir.

Though they wanted to respect the house's vernacular, and to use pieces inherited from Casa Bendita, which Addison Mizner built for Jay's grandfather John S. Phipps in 1921, the Cochrans had no desire for formal or period interiors. They called upon longtime friend interior designer Jeff Lincoln, who has created interiors for houses designed by Fatio, Stanford White, and Mott Schmidt. His clients include ambassadors, news anchors, and Baseball Hall of Fame chairman Jane Forbes Clark, for whom he designed personal residences and the Otesaga Hotel in Cooperstown.

"The mandate was for a comfortable home for a young family," Lincoln says. "Key pieces of furniture, art, and family heirlooms provided the basis of the design, combined with a love for the style and sensibility of Fortuny fabrics used in a modern, elegant way." He designed commodious furniture to establish a relaxed and unpretentious atmosphere. A palette of slate blues, earthy oranges, and powdery whites contributes both verve and serenity. Contemporary art, including photographs by family friends Peter Beard, Horst, and Bruce Weber, and furniture by George Nakashima mix harmoniously with classical pieces.

The family's penchant for collecting extends to the outdoors. Jay collaborated with friend and garden designer Nathan Browning, of Island Planning Corporation, who started his career working for Rem Koolhaas and now designs projects for Aman Resorts, LVMH, and private clients from Panama and Greece to Vietnam and Montenegro. The men began procuring palm trees endemic to Cuba and the broader Caribbean, eventually amassing an impressive collection of species, including *Copernicia fallense*, *Copernicia baileyana*, *Copernicia hospita*, *Coccothrinax crinita*, *Coccothrinax miraguama*, and *Sabal domingensis*, which punctuate the massive lawn like sculptures. "Jay's garden is not full of hedges and flower beds, but is an artistic composition where the plants have a good relationship with one another," says Browning. Tucked in among the trees are whimsical sculptures by Jay's mother, Susie Phipps Cochran, who lives nearby, surrounded by a junglelike garden.

"My mother-in-law calls this the grown-up house," admits Diahann. In truth, the Cochrans managed to combine pedigree architecture, furniture, and plantings in a way that creates the comfortable family home they envisioned.

OPPOSITE: Maurice Fatio was hailed for his striking entrance halls. The table originally graced Casa Bendita, designed by Addison Mizner for John S. Phipps.

ABOVE: On the loggia, the earthy orange Fortuny fabric used for cushions and pillows takes on a fresh look in combination with furnishings upholstered in raffia from Hinson & Company. A custom braided rug from Stark and sheer linen curtains add to the loggia's airy feeling.

OVERLEAF: A poolside loggia, conveniently serviced by a small outdoor kitchen to the left, is a favorite gathering spot. *Phoenix sylvestris* palms are reflected in the mirror.

TOP LEFT: Terra-cotta pots planted with *Alcantarea imperialis* bromeliads dot the pool area.

TOP RIGHT: A towering *Copernicia baileyana* adds visual interest to a walkway from the main house to the outdoor loggia.

ABOVE LEFT: The pool is surrounded with grass for softness underfoot.

ABOVE RIGHT: *Coccothrinax* palms frame a whimsical sculpture by Susie Phipps Cochran.

OPPOSITE: Massive *Phoenix sylvestris* palms sway over chaises longues, providing shade overhead.

OPPOSITE: A custom settee from Jonas, upholstered in Rogers & Goffigon fabric, flooring by Waterworks, and a pretty view combine to turn the master bath into a retreat.

RIGHT: A window in the master bedroom overlooks the pool and the owner's beloved collection of Cuban and Caribbean palm trees. Curtains of Rogers & Goffigon linen are bordered with a Fortuny fabric.

BELOW: A palm-themed scenic wallpaper by Gracie creates a calm setting. The bed is from Robert Lighton's British Khaki collection, and the zebra-print ottoman is from Wilson Antiques on Dixie Highway. The desk in the foreground was fashioned by Jay Cochran, who is an accomplished furniture maker.

INHERENT BEAUTY

Pauline Pitt's storied ancestry exemplifies the belief of Arts and Crafts movement founder William Morris that beauty unites generations. This lineage of splendor—at least in house design—began in the 1920s, when Pitt's paternal grandfather, George F. Baker Jr., son of a founder of the bank that eventually became Citibank, commissioned architectural firm Delano & Aldrich to construct a complex of townhouses at 93rd Street and Park Avenue, the highest point in Manhattan. The plan included the ultimate in luxury, a railroad spur in the basement to connect the family's private railroad car with the underground Park Avenue line. The complex's mansion is now occupied by the Russian Orthodox Church Outside of Russia. Preservationist Richard Jenrette owns the smaller home, and the Classical American Homes Preservation Trust operates out of the former carriage house.

The Baker family spent weekends on Long Island's North Shore in a Delano & Aldrich Georgian-style house with interiors by Syrie Maugham, a leading British decorator of the 1920s and 1930s. Maugham was known for rooms decorated entirely in blinding intensities of white.

In 1919 Pitt's maternal grandparents, Charles and Mary Munn, commissioned Addison Mizner to design their Palm Beach house, the iconic Amado. Charles Munn's charming manner and tall, dark good looks earned him the title "Mr. Palm Beach," and Mizner, the era's most famous resort architect, known for his Mediterranean and Spanish Colonial Revival designs, including the Everglades Club, gave him a house worthy of his moniker.

Pitt's mother, Frances Drexel Munn Baker, commissioned a house at the tip of Centre Island on Long Island in the style of a French manor. The elegance of the formal entrance hall, with its curved staircase and floor of 24-by-24-inch black and red marble tiles had a profound impact on Pitt, as did the Baker family's Horseshoe Plantation in northern Florida, a sprawling and stylish house designed by Palm Beach's preeminent post-Mizner architect, John Volk.

OPPOSITE: A gate at the front entrance provides security yet permits breezes to waft in. An enormous ficus tree shades the gravel entrance court. The oxidized copper lantern has taken on a pretty green cast.

ABOVE: Espaliered orange trees and potted kumquat trees adorn the façade of the house. Capable of withstanding extreme temperatures, ranging from a high of 100°F to a low of 14°F, kumquats are often used decoratively in Florida.

Given her heritage, it's no surprise that Pitt became an interior designer. Her aesthetic leans toward charming and cozy, perhaps in reaction to her formal upbringing but more likely garnered from the experience of co-owning a trendy design shop in London with Colefax and Fowler disciple Jane Churchill in the early 1970s. After years spent designing many Palm Beach homes for clients and a few for herself, Pitt was ready to put her stamp on a permanent Palm Beach residence that came with her marriage in 2000 to William Pitt, chairman of William Pitt Real Estate in Stamford, Connecticut. When Pauline first saw the house, she loved the setting—not only was it on Lake Worth but it was also directly west of her family's oceanfront home, Amado. But the bachelor pad was in sore need of a transformation. "It was the type of situation where if you plugged in a blow dryer, all the fuses would blow out," Pitt says with her infectious laugh.

Because this house was going to be her permanent residence, Pitt's mandate was to enlarge it to accommodate a seasonally convivial lifestyle yet not sacrifice the coziness of the original layout. Most important, Pauline wanted to imbue the place with gentility and a sense of calm and ease, the same qualities she loves about Palm Beach living.

She opted not to enlarge the footprint but to build up, creating a second story for a master bedroom that offers sweeping views of the Intracoastal Waterway and the West Palm Beach skyline. And she turned the original master bedroom on the main floor into a sumptuous guest room. First impressions are everything, so Pitt gave the house a welcoming soft pink façade trimmed with white shutters and trained vines that exudes her hospitable personality.

For the interiors, Pauline created a balanced mix of old and new, formal and casual. Wicker and lattice set a laid-back tropical tone in the dining room and on the patio; other rooms feature inherited antiques and art, including a painting of her mother by Salvador Dalí. In the living room, pecky cypress paneling lends a distinctly casual Florida touch, while a cloudy white wool rug bound in white leather adds an element of formality. White furniture was a natural choice for a Florida family room, but but Pitt boldly decided to paint the walls a deep navy blue, which sets off the furniture and provides a dramatic backdrop for inherited Chinese pieces.

Two rooms were joined to create a spacious dining room with several seating areas so it can hold a large number of guests and yet still feel intimate; from November to April the house buzzes with activity. At one time, Palm Beach's social stratification was clearly defined, and Pauline's maternal grandparents undeniably occupied the top rung. Today, there are many overlapping social circles, but Pitt remains at the epicenter. She welcomes visits from her two daughters and their growing families, as well as extended family and friends. Even when her house is full of people, which is more often than not, it never feels cramped or overcrowded. "What I love about this house is that it is cozy with lots of nooks and crannies—I can have two hundred people for a party and it still feels intimate," says Pitt, who continues the family legacy of uniting generations through beauty.

Walls in a delicate shade of pink, lush shrubbery, trained vines, and white shutters soften the stucco and brick façade. The neighboring house was purchased to make room for a cutting garden, the entrance of which is marked by two fanciful stone frogs.

OPPOSITE: Bob Christian of Savannah, Georgia, took four days to paint the entrance hall's whimsical mural, setting an inviting tone for guests.

ABOVE: Decorative items, including a clock purchased in England, inherited silver ashtrays, and a Ming figurine are scattered throughout the house. A dark wooden mirror was painted white to suit its subtropical setting.

TOP TO BOTTOM: A decorative parrot and three monogrammed silver ashtrays inlaid with silver coins, which Pitt's great-uncle Gurnee Munn gave to family members as Christmas presents. Pitt uses them as table decorations and wine coasters.

Livingston Builders of Palm Beach salvaged the mantel from the nearby Vanderbilt estate. Hanging above it is Salvador Dalí's portrait of Pauline's mother, Frances Munn Baker.

TOP AND ABOVE: White furniture and inherited Chinese art pop against the dramatic navy blue walls of the family room, which opens into the dining room.

TOP LEFT: A set of silver cutlery, circa 1919, from the nearby Munn family residence, Amado, is engraved *M.M.* for Mary Munn.

ABOVE LEFT: Blue-and-white Tiffany china echoes the dining room's color scheme.

TOP RIGHT: The Chinese sconces are from John Rosselli Antiques.

ABOVE RIGHT: Dessert is served on Dodie Thayer's handmade pottery, a Palm Beach classic.

RIGHT: White lattice over blue walls gives the dining room an airy, tropical feeling. A window seat covered in a Bennison fabric provides extra seating.

LEFT: The guest bedroom opens onto the pool area and has a view of Lake Worth. An ethereal Manuel Canovas fabric is used for the headboard, canopy, chair, and curtains. A pillow reads: "All our guests bring happiness. Some by coming, others by going."

BELOW: Desk accessories, including an antique shaving mirror, export china, and a papier-mâché tray, give the room a cozy English feeling.

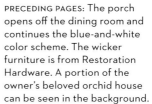

PRECEDING PAGES: The porch opens off the dining room and continues the blue-and-white color scheme. The wicker furniture is from Restoration Hardware. A portion of the owner's beloved orchid house can be seen in the background.

ABOVE: Breakfast is served on Hermès china. Fragrant gardenias from the owner's garden decorate the table.

TOP: A quirky dish enlivens a side table.

ABOVE: A traditional garden stool in the shape of an elephant serves as a side table.

OPPOSITE: The covered porch is the perfect spot for breakfast and afternoon iced tea. The outdoor dining furniture is from Brown Jordan.

GARDENS
AND POOLS

PALM BEACH'S ORIGINAL LANDSCAPE SCHEME TOOK root in 1878, when the Spanish brigantine *Providencia*, carrying a cargo of twenty thousand coconuts, was wrecked offshore. Early settlers planted the seeds, creating a palm-filled landscape that gave the area its name and continues to dominate the town's horticultural ambience.

The Garden Club of Palm Beach was organized in 1928, and by the next year there were forty-three members, whose interest was centered on preserving Lake Trail, which was considered an important part of old Palm Beach. Their next project was to commission a plan for the Town of Palm Beach. Garden Club members contributed the entire $10,000 to pay for the plan, which was completed and presented to the town in 1930. In 1935 the proceeds of a successful flower show enabled the club to plant three blocks of Royal Palm Way with royal palms. Since then, the club has continuously been involved with the beautification of Palm Beach, renewing and enhancing its public spaces. Recent projects include commissioning the planting of South Ocean Boulevard's new roundabout, contributing design expertise and financial backing for Worth Avenue's Living Wall, and supporting the replanting of Poinciana Plaza with kaleidoscope flower beds.

The Society of the Four Arts Demonstration Garden, adjacent to the town library, is considered the Garden Club's most important achievement; it is a template for garden design in the South Florida climate. Open year round and free of charge to the public since 1939, the garden consists of nine diverse landscape schemes (including the Chinese Garden, Jungle Garden, Moonlight Garden, Formal Garden, and Spanish Façade) designed and donated by five Garden Club members.

The private gardens shown here are intimate places created to frame a pool, provide shade and respite, or extend living areas beyond four walls. Human in scale, they are as varied in form as their inhabitants and the notable landscape architects who designed them.

OPPOSITE: The Hunts enjoy breakfast on the loggia that overlooks the garden. Fernando Tonarely hand-glazed the walls in a pale butter color.

ABOVE: A detail of the hand-carved screen that hangs on the loggia wall. The screen, from India, was found in an antiques store on Dixie Highway.

PRIVACY AMONG THE HEDGES

When planning their Palm Beach house, Terry and John Rakolta envisioned it as a balmy retreat from Michigan winters as well as a hideaway where Terry could relax between archaeological digs in Egypt, Honduras, and points in between. They dreamed of an expansive lawn alongside a waterway, where they could enjoy watching painted sunsets and boats passing by. But upon moving in, they realized that the sweeping lawn lacked focal points and that they were more viewed than doing the viewing. "Boats would anchor right in front of our house and watch us swim. We were so exposed. It was unnerving," says Terry.

The Rakoltas called on garden designer Jorge Sánchez to solve the privacy issue. He suggested planting walls of ficus hedges to section the lawn into three areas: a pool "room" screened from boat traffic by a curtain of ashoka trees; a separate dining area, referred to as the "cathedral," the ground covered with pebbles to support table and chairs; and a smaller, more intimate lawn. "Jorge managed to save our view, blending water, pool, and sky so thoroughly that no element dominates."

TOP: A trellis-framed mirror was tucked into the hedge to reflect the pool.

ABOVE LEFT: The finial-topped pillar of the entrance gate establishes a formal tone.

ABOVE RIGHT: An allée of medjool date palms frames a view of West Palm Beach in the garden's dining "cathedral."

OPPOSITE: Arched "doorways" in the ficus hedges permit a view from the lawn to the swimming pool and beyond to the dining cathedral, where the trellis-framed mirror creates a false perspective.

OVERLEAF: The swimming pool was lined with hedges to create intimacy and to separate the lawn and the dining area. A row of ashoka trees frames the water and the sky while offering privacy and obstructing the less desirable view of West Palm Beach's high rises.

OPPOSITE: In the 20-by-40-foot greenhouse, slats are positioned to allow indirect sunlight and air circulation for the plants. Despite its airy appearance, the greenhouse conforms to Florida's hurricane code and can withstand 117-mile-an-hour winds.

THIS PAGE: A sampling of the 200 orchid varieties Kit Pannill coaxes to bloom during the winter months.

OVERLEAF: An enormous *Ficus benjamina* is the centerpiece of the north garden. When the Pannills first acquired the house, the tree was small and a nearby shed had a hole in the roof. Panill left the tree to its own devices but transformed the shed into a delightful pool house. The Flagler Museum can be seen in the distance.

TROPICAL PARADISE

When asked to describe a favorite spot in his Palm Beach garden, the charismatic Leonard Lauder says, "I love my outdoor shower; I love sitting at the pool and looking at the beautifully sculptured cypress trees; I love sitting on the patio and listening to music; I love it everywhere."

Lauder's cherished gardens surround one of Palm Beach's most iconic houses: a Beaux-Arts-style mansion, designed in 1938 by Marion Sims Wyeth and purchased in 1964 by the late cosmetics queen Estée Lauder and her husband, Joe, ever after associating Palm Beach with the Lauder name. Everyone slows down to admire the white columned and pedimented façade at the foot of North Ocean Boulevard.

Townspeople and tourists alike still refer to it as "Estée Lauder's house," but when she retired and began spending most of her time in New York, she turned it over to her eldest son, Leonard, and his late wife, Evelyn. Leonard's younger brother, Ronald, lives next door in an equally beautiful Mediterranean Revival home, also designed by Wyeth.

ABOVE: Detail of the seahorse-and-shell motif on cast-iron outdoor furniture painted frosted rose.

OPPOSITE: One of Palm Beach's most beloved façades, designed in 1938 by Marion Sims Wyeth. The house, once owned by Joseph and Estée Lauder, and still referred to by locals as "Estée's house," was passed along to her son Leonard Lauder.

Like Estée before her, Evelyn considered the Palm Beach home a family retreat. For Estée that meant formal lunches and dinners in the dining room, whereas for Evelyn and Leonard it meant relaxed meals outdoors and multigenerational parties on the sweeping ocean-side lawn, complete with climbing walls and bouncy castles.

With Estée's blessing, Evelyn created a more casual atmosphere under the guidance of architect Jeff Smith and interior designer Thad Hayes, choosing linens and cottons where there used to be silks, and merging indoors and outdoors to create a more tropical experience. When Evelyn turned her famously discerning eye toward the grounds, she realized that, compared to the newly relaxed interiors, the plantings appeared starchy. She wanted to envelop the house in greenery and called upon landscape designer Mario Nievera.

"She and Leonard had the good fortune of meeting Brazilian garden designer Roberto Burle Marx. Evelyn was very taken with his big-scale, sexy, tropical designs," says Nievera. "We went all around and picked out plants. She knew about everything."

One of Evelyn's mandates was to make the long-ignored northern edge of the property more accessible and inviting. Nievera created a walkway lined with towering sago palms, screw pines, ti plants, and bamboo, reminiscent of a tropical jungle. The families use the path as a shortcut between the two houses, as well as to the nearby Breakers hotel. The most important new element tucked into the jungle, however, is an outdoor shower, used on the way home from the beach. "One of the great but simple pleasures of life is to shower outside and be able to see the sky," reflects Leonard Lauder.

OVERLEAF: The outdoor furniture on the east terrace is maintained with "wet" paint, which withstands the elements. When the Lauders entertain for dinner, one very long, narrow table is set, ensuring that everyone is seated with the host and can converse easily. This arrangement is the Lauders' signature.

TOP, LEFT TO RIGHT: Conceived by Evelyn Lauder and Mario Nievera, Leonard Lauder's beloved outdoor shower is hidden along the jungle walk; a gently trickling fountain decorates the interior courtyard and is softened with plantings; when the ocean winds whip up, lunch is served in the protected interior courtyard.

ABOVE: To give the narrow walk that serves as a path to the beach and to the family's other house—also designed by Marion Sims Wyeth and owned by Leonard Lauder's brother, Ronald—its junglelike effect, garden designer Mario Nievera lined it with dramatic screw pines, sago palms, ti plants, elephant ears, bamboo, and birds of paradise,

OPPOSITE: A pathway near the interior courtyard leads to the pool, which is surrounded by towering hedges and climbing bougainvillea.

INTERNATIONAL HIGH STYLE

A VERITABLE TROPICAL JUNGLE OBSCURES THE ENTRANCE to the soaring limestone oceanfront villa designed by architect Thierry Despont, making its appearance all that much more dramatic when it looms into view. One part shelter, three parts sculpture, it's no wonder that the École des Beaux-Arts- and Harvard-trained Despont is also an accomplished visual artist. His 2012 New York exhibition, *Le Cabinet de Curiosités*, a collaboration with Marlborough Galleries and storied Parisian antiques dealer Steinitz, was a curated combination of contemporary art and antiques that introduced thousands of viewers to the inner reaches of Despont's lithe and seemingly limitless imagination. In the case of this house, Despont's mediums included limestone, mahogany, and five hundred thousand curated pebbles from Mexico's Pacific coast to pave the driveway.

Despont is known for translating the vision of clients such as Bill Gates, Millard "Mickey" Drexler, and Calvin Klein—men who are famous for dreaming big— into brick-and-mortar realities beyond their wildest dreams. In this case the client, Sidney Kimmel, founder of Jones Apparel Group, requested a central atrium. Not surprisingly, what Despont delivered was a space that leaves all who enter breathless.

Twenty-six feet high and 32 feet long, the atrium's transparent ceiling is lined with 34 enormous curved beams of Honduran mahogany, each 115 feet long. Resembling the hull of an ancient Phoenician galley, the wooden "sculpture" was commissioned from a shipbuilder in Pensacola, Florida, who took nearly a year to fulfill the unusual request. On one side of the room are six twenty-foot-high mahogany-framed glass doors; with a push of a button, they disappear into the ground, creating an open-air pavilion that overlooks an infinity pool and the Atlantic Ocean to the east and formal gardens with a swimming pool and other water features to the west.

Naturally, this atrium is what first impressed the new owners, who had been looking for a primary residence in Palm Beach for three years. "We wanted a small house

OPPOSITE: High above the atrium are 34 curved beams of Honduran mahogany, each 115 feet long, commissioned from a Pensacola, Florida, shipbuilder.

ABOVE: Detail of the palm frond–patterned tiles on an exterior wall behind the dining room.

The pebbled driveway
is reflected in one of the
glass doors.

on the ocean, so we were more than surprised by our reaction to this house. It's not small, but it's very Zen. The views and vistas are so many and strong that you feel as if you are always outside, which we love," says the wife.

The owners were also swayed by the fact that house was not only in perfect condition but was also delivered furnished, as most Despont houses are. "Despont designed the house on a very large scale, and much of the furniture was also designed by him. We had never bought a house that could be moved into right away. We have lived in a number of different cities, and most of the houses in which we settled were old and a bit of a wreck and needed major restoration work."

Despont designed the five-acre geometric garden to have a strong correspondence to the house. Built along a strong east–west axis, the garden has been described as suggesting the different phases of life, beginning with a large, grass-surrounded circular fountain, then down a rill to another garden room and fountain, and eventually on out to the horizon. The only changes the couple made to the landscape were the addition of palms to the front lawn to soften the light and the removal of plantings that obscured the view of the ocean.

PRECEDING PAGES: The infinity pool is lined with blue Murano glass. The overhang continues the thrust of the mahogany beams that span the atrium, creating a powerful connection between the interior and the exterior.

ABOVE: The architect, Thierry Despont, is also a visual artist, and many of the views are wonderfully framed.

OPPOSITE: Twin stairways lead to a family room and to the master suite. Despont designed the living room and library furniture in perfect proportion to the size of these grand rooms.

OVERLEAF: The dining room and the entrance hall are on either side of the atrium. Bamboo growing in planters blurs the lines between indoors and out.

OPPOSITE: The wife, a distinguished author, is an avid reader.

ABOVE: An outdoor dining table overlooking the pool on the western side of the house is protected from the ocean winds.

OVERLEAF: On one side of the atrium, six mahogany-framed glass doors, each twenty feet high, can disappear into the ground, turning the house into an open-air pavilion.

PAGES 296–97: The gardens, also designed by Despont, unify the house with its setting. Water features, including fountains and pools, create a sense of otherworldliness.

OLD BETHESDA-BY-THE-SEA

Palm Beach native Mimi Kemble McMakin's design company, Kemble Interiors, is responsible for the redecoration of some of America's most storied houses and private clubs. With offices in Palm Beach, New York, and London, McMakin is constantly traveling the world to oversee her myriad projects, yet never loses focus on the necessary, often inconspicuous minutiae that ensure that her beloved clients always have not only stylish surroundings but also handy places to set a drink and plug in a phone.

Ironically, nothing is quite so meticulous about McMakin's own residence, including the fact that she lives in a former church that was absorbed into her family's lakeside compound in the early 1940s, when the congregation moved to what is now Bethesda-by-the-Sea.

McMakin grew up next door to the church, shuttering her bedroom windows against its gloomy façade. As an adult, she moved to New York to pursue a design career but returned regularly to the family compound. During one visit, she discovered that tenants had vacated the church and promptly moved in; a short stay turned into a lifetime, and more than forty years later, she's still excavating the church nave, which had become a catch-all of oddities discarded by generations of free spirits. "Try telling someone you are a designer with butterflies, zebras, snakes, alligators, Fabio posters, parrots, porcupines, a model of the sinking *Titanic*, whales, giraffes, and a canoe living in your house." No matter how much she clears out, more finds its way in. "Someone left an oversized stuffed giraffe on our doorstep one Christmas, so we added it to the collection," she recalls. "A former business partner saw a twelve-foot-wide butterfly kite in Napa Valley and thought I had to have it. Now it hangs from our rafters."

Though there are proper bedrooms, and a long loggia at the back of the house is arranged as a living room, the nave remains an all-purpose room. When Mimi's two daughters, Celerie and Phoebe, were young, everything was pushed aside so they could skateboard and play house. For a goddaughter's rehearsal dinner, McMakin created a mini-Venice, snaking long tables topped with gondola centerpieces through the

OPPOSITE: The former Bethesda-by-the-Sea Episcopal Church, whose last service was held on Easter Sunday, April 12, 1925, has been a private residence in the pioneer Maddock family for five generations. The steeple's Seth Thomas clock is original. The family often gathers on the western lawn to watch the sunset.

ABOVE: A detail of the Portuguese tile floor in the sunroom.

OPPOSITE: Jack Russell terriers Turtle and Anchovie greet visitors on the front steps of the sunroom.

ABOVE: A hand-painted sign marks the entrance of the house. Mimi Maddock McMakin and her daughters, Celerie and Phoebe Kemble, represent the fifth and sixth generations with ties to the church.

RIGHT: The bell tower of the church steeple is visible from the front of the house.

room, which was decorated with jauntily striped gondola poles. Not surprisingly, some of the poles remain and have been added to the "permanent collection." Whatever its existing arrangement, the nave is always a playroom for McMakin's visiting grandchildren, whose favorite game is to count the number of animals hidden in the décor.

When the entire family is in residence, Mimi's husband, Leigh, refers to the church as "The Asylum." He has become loyal to his wife's family house, going so far as to tack down the vines that surround the steeple in the middle of rainstorms. Everyone takes the constant upkeep in stride, even the water leak that turned out to be honey: a beehive was discovered in the wall.

As it did to Mimi forty years ago, the house takes hold of anyone or anything that has the good fortune to enter. Its design may be serendipitous, but there is always a place to set down a drink, although, as is true of most eighteenth-century buildings, working outlets are hardly abundant. But when a phone dies, it hardly matters; texting is no competition for the view of the lake from beneath a clock tower that has dazzled passersby for over a century.

LEFT: One enters the house through the sunroom, where wooden floors were replaced with cheerful Portuguese tile, and the walls were painted pale pink; they were so porous that it took five coats of paint to camouflage the original dark brown shingles. The wicker furniture has been glazed green. McMakin has replaced the fabric only three times in thirty-five years. Two enormous fiddle leaf fig trees frame the door and prosper in the sunlight.

ABOVE: A portrait of Lucy Lacoste Maddock, who was married to McMakin's great-grandfather Sydney Maddock—owner of the former Palm Beach Hotel—at age eighteen. She swam across the Intracoastal Waterway daily.

OVERLEAF: The historic church is situated along Palm Beach's bike path and affords views of the Intracoastal Waterway and the West Palm Beach skyline beyond. When the church was built at the turn of the twentieth century, worshipers arrived by boat from the mainland. as there was only marshland to the now-developed east. The pineapple lantern, designed by McMakin, is one of the lighting fixtures offered in her shop, Kemble Interiors, on Hibiscus Way. Over the years, family descendants have pressed their handprints into the concrete walkway.

OPPOSITE AND ABOVE LEFT: A loggia running along the western side of the house serves as a living room and gallery and features generations of family treasures, including a whale from McMakin's mother's house in Northeast Harbor, Maine; watercolor studies by McMakin's daughter interior designer Celerie Kemble; a good-luck pig carried home from Bangkok; a red chinoiserie screen brought home from China in the 1800s by McMakin's great-grandmother Jeannie Maddock; and a canoe called "Little Lassie," found in the Adirondacks. The floral fabric covering the furniture is from Colefax and Fowler.

ABOVE RIGHT: In the master bedroom, the wooden floor is glazed in a green-and-white diamond pattern. The loveseat belonged to McMakin's great-grandmother Jeannie Maddock. Rather than leave it in storage, McMakin bravely whitewashed it. The arched section of the window is made of sea glass, which creates dappled light. The portrait is of McMakin's daughter Phoebe.

OVERLEAF: The church's original nave remains as it was when the church was built in 1894. The church was deconsecrated in the mid-1920s and became part of the Maddock family compound shortly thereafter. Ever since, the nave has been a catch-all of oddities that McMakin has been excavating and augmenting during her forty-year residence. A portrait of Leigh McMakin's mother, Martha Ashley McMakin, hangs in the center of the back wall. On the far left is a portrait of Lucy Lacoste Maddock. The parasols are from Bangkok, and the twelve-foot butterfly kite is from Napa, California. The alligator is a prototype for a coffee table requested by a client. The angels are from the Dominican Republic. The gondola poles on the right were acquired for a Venice-themed rehearsal dinner. The mahogany gambling table on the far left is from Bradley's Beach Club, built in 1898. A sisal rug was painted to look like an Aubusson.

ACKNOWLEDGMENTS

THIS BOOK OWES EVERYTHING TO THE EXPERT GUIDANCE of everyone at Vendome Press. Special thanks to Mark Magowan, who steered the project from start to finish with care and creativity. His discerning eye ensured the book's splendor. Nina Magowan was a superb sounding board and thoughtful advisor. I'm most grateful to my editor, Jackie Decter, whose sound judgment, sure sense of proportion, and ever-present sense of humor made every stage of the process a delight. Her tenacious fact checking is the first, second, and third line of defense against inaccuracies on these pages. Designer Celia Fuller magically turned vague notions into a fresh and glorious design. I am thankful to Alexis Gregory for his encouragement and invaluable comments.

The beauty of this book depended on the remarkable talent of photographer Jessica Klewicki Glynn; her diligence and unflappability turned long days of photographing into a rare pleasure.

I would be completely lost without the perspective, care, and wit of my mother, Agnes Ash. She's an easy-going high achiever who taught me that there's value in hard work and pleasure in collaboration. I'd like to thank my children, Clarke and Amelia, for always weighing in and holding down the fort in New York while I was in Florida. A heartfelt thanks to my husband, Joe—he remains unfailingly supportive of my pursuits, and his limitless energy and optimism always carry the day.

I must extend special thanks to Lillian Fernandez, whose friendship and interest in this project gave me the confidence to see it through and opened more than a few doors. Patty Norris's mere presence was a reminder that genuine hospitality and old-fashioned graciousness still exist.

Finally, I am deeply grateful to all those who pointed us in the right direction and to the owners and the designers of the singular houses and gardens on these pages. They gave freely of their time and trusted us with their stories. There would be no book without the kindness of Cece Abrams, Jackie Albarran, Iris and Carl Apfel, Alexander and Nancy von Auersperg, Debbie and Anson Beard, Lars and Nadine

Bolander, Meg Braff, Lori Deeds, Nathan Browning, Jay and Diahann Cochran, Paige Crawford, Lori Deeds, Margo and Ashton de Peyster, Beth DeWoody, Tiffany Dubin, David Easton, Mark Ferguson, Leta Foster, Jennifer Garrigues, Cobus Gauche, Wayne Giancaterino, Mary Hilliard, Jane and Michael Horvitz, Vicky Hunt, Patrick Killian, David Kleinberg, Terry Allen Kramer, Patrick Killian, Tom Kirchhoff, Kelly Klein, Bill Kopp, John Lang, Leonard Lauder, William Lauder, Jeff Lincoln, Peter Marino, Sally Marks, Mimi and Leigh McMakin, Keithley Miller, Dani Hickox Moore, Peggy Moore, Christina Murphy, Lucy Musso, Josie Natori, Mario Nievera, Fernanda Niven, Polly Norris, Jean Pearman, Michael Peasley, William and Ida Pencer, Lisa Perry, Pauline Pitt, Liza Pulitzer, Peter Pulitzer, Terry Rakolta, Kathy and Billy Rayner, Rob and Julie Revely, Burke Ross, Crista Ryan, Jorge and Serina Phipps Sánchez, Harry and Laura Slatkin, Jeff Smith, Jeff Stemes, Alan Stopek, John and Margaret Thornton, Calvin Tsao, Alexis Waller, and Keith Williams.

—Jennifer Ash Rudick

 I WOULD FIRST LIKE TO THANK JENNIFER ASH RUDICK FOR recognizing my talent, gaining access to extraordinary homes, and using her keen eye to style shoots. I am deeply grateful to publisher Mark Magowan for putting his faith in my photographic skills. Thank you also to editor Jackie Decter and designer Celia Fuller for making the book flow beautifully.

My contribution to the book would not have been possible without the support of my husband, Gerard Glynn. He has always been my pillar of strength and the greatest champion of my career and art. Thank you to my mother and father, Gail and Ray Klewicki. Their extreme generosity and willingness to assist me in any and all ways never ceases to amaze me. They inspired me to "dream big." And they cared for my little girl, Keira, when Mommy had to work. Thank you, Keira, for making me a stronger and better person. Thank you to *all* of my family and friends, who have always been so supportive and caring. Thank you to my mentors, teachers, clients, prop stylist, and photo retouchers: Frank Martucci, Deborah Arvanitis-Dunigan, Tom Ang, Norman Moyes, Caroline Metcalfe at Condé Nast Traveller UK, Olivia O'Bryan Inc., Laurin Lott and the Windsor Club, Clemens Bruns Schaub Architects, Corey Weiner, Dana Hoff, Claudia Miyar, Krissy Taylor-Costea, and Michael Warnock. And thank you to all of the homeowners, interior designers, architects, and caretakers for welcoming us and preparing their beautiful homes for us.

—Jessica Klewicki Glynn

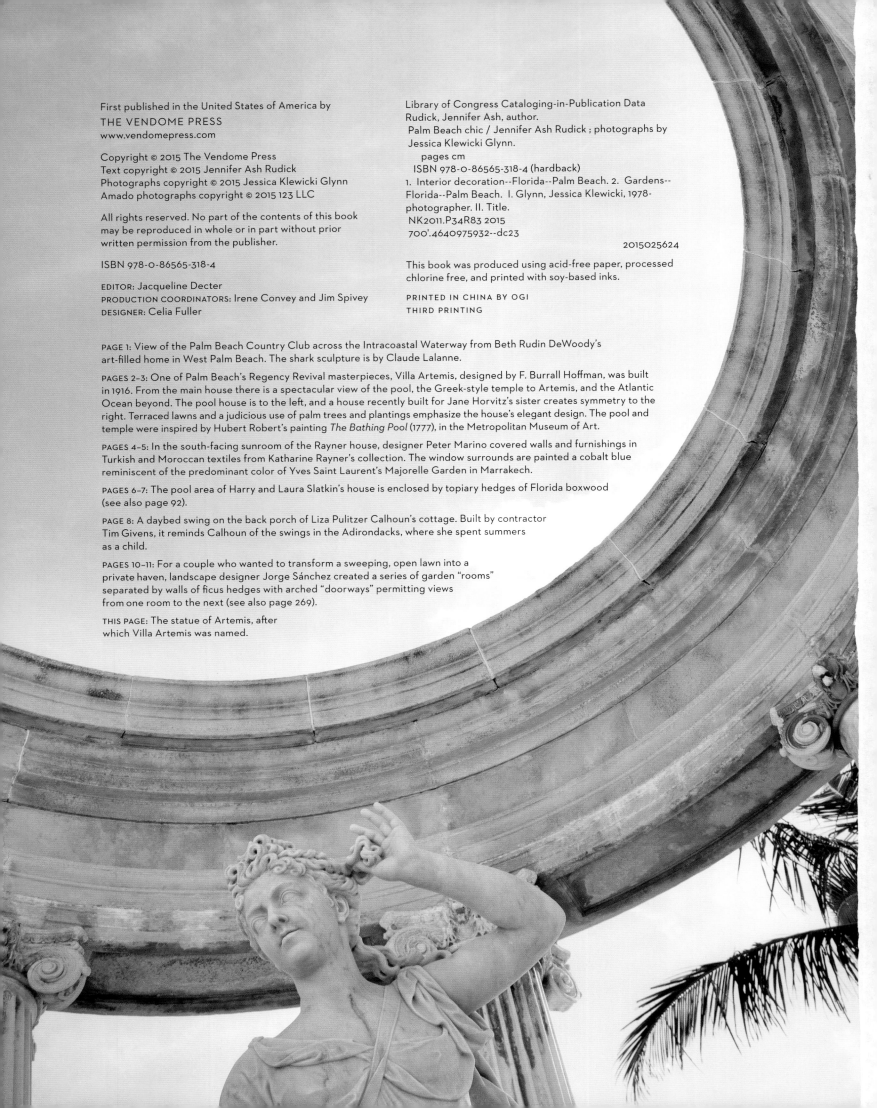

First published in the United States of America by
THE VENDOME PRESS
www.vendomepress.com

ISBN 978-0-86565-318-4

EDITOR: Jacqueline Decter
PRODUCTION COORDINATORS: Irene Convey and Jim Spivey
DESIGNER: Celia Fuller

Library of Congress Cataloging-in-Publication Data
Rudick, Jennifer Ash, author.
 Palm Beach chic / Jennifer Ash Rudick ; photographs by
 Jessica Klewicki Glynn.
   pages cm
  ISBN 978-0-86565-318-4 (hardback)
1. Interior decoration--Florida--Palm Beach. 2. Gardens--
Florida--Palm Beach. I. Glynn, Jessica Klewicki, 1978-
photographer. II. Title.
 NK2011.P34R83 2015
 700'.4640975932--dc23
                                                  2015025624

This book was produced using acid-free paper, processed
chlorine free, and printed with soy-based inks.

PRINTED IN CHINA BY OGI
THIRD PRINTING

PAGE 1: View of the Palm Beach Country Club across the Intracoastal Waterway from Beth Rudin DeWoody's art-filled home in West Palm Beach. The shark sculpture is by Claude Lalanne.

PAGES 2–3: One of Palm Beach's Regency Revival masterpieces, Villa Artemis, designed by F. Burrall Hoffman, was built in 1916. From the main house there is a spectacular view of the pool, the Greek-style temple to Artemis, and the Atlantic Ocean beyond. The pool house is to the left, and a house recently built for Jane Horvitz's sister creates symmetry to the right. Terraced lawns and a judicious use of palm trees and plantings emphasize the house's elegant design. The pool and temple were inspired by Hubert Robert's painting *The Bathing Pool* (1777), in the Metropolitan Museum of Art.

PAGES 4–5: In the south-facing sunroom of the Rayner house, designer Peter Marino covered walls and furnishings in Turkish and Moroccan textiles from Katharine Rayner's collection. The window surrounds are painted a cobalt blue reminiscent of the predominant color of Yves Saint Laurent's Majorelle Garden in Marrakech.

PAGES 6–7: The pool area of Harry and Laura Slatkin's house is enclosed by topiary hedges of Florida boxwood (see also page 92).

PAGE 8: A daybed swing on the back porch of Liza Pulitzer Calhoun's cottage. Built by contractor Tim Givens, it reminds Calhoun of the swings in the Adirondacks, where she spent summers as a child.

PAGES 10–11: For a couple who wanted to transform a sweeping, open lawn into a private haven, landscape designer Jorge Sánchez created a series of garden "rooms" separated by walls of ficus hedges with arched "doorways" permitting views from one room to the next (see also page 269).

THIS PAGE: The statue of Artemis, after which Villa Artemis was named.